Doing App

GW00585653

Doing Applied Linguistics provides a concise, lively and accessible introduction to the field of applied linguistics for readers who have little or no prior knowledge of the subject. The book explores the basics of the field then goes on to examine in more depth what applied linguists actually do, and the types of research methods that are most frequently used in the field. By reading this book students will find answers to four sets of basic questions:

- What is applied linguistics, and what do applied linguists do?
- Why do it? What is the point of applied linguistics?
- How and why might I get involved in applied linguistics?
- How to do it? What kinds of activities are involved in doing applied linguistic research?

Written by teachers and researchers in applied linguistics *Doing Applied Linguistics* is essential reading for all students with interests in this area.

The e-resource can be found at:
www.routledge.com/9780415566421

Nicholas Groom is lecturer in Applied Linguistics at the University of Birmingham, UK.

Jeannette Littlemore is senior lecturer in Applied Linguistics at the University of Birmingham, UK.

Doing Applied Linguistics

A Guide for Students

*Nicholas Groom and
Jeannette Littlemore*

Routledge
Taylor & Francis Group

LONDON AND NEW YORK

First published 2011
by Routledge
2 Park Square, Milton Park, Abingdon, Oxon OX14 4RN

Simultaneously published in the USA and Canada
by Routledge
711 Third Avenue, New York, NY 10017

Routledge is an imprint of the Taylor & Francis Group, an informa business

British Library Cataloguing in Publication Data
A catalogue record for this book is available from the British Library

Library of Congress Cataloging in Publication Data
Groom, Nicholas.
Doing applied linguistics : a guide for students /
Nicholas Groom and Jeannette Littlemore.
p. cm.
Includes bibliographical references and index.
1. Applied linguistics. I. Littlemore, Jeannette. II. Title.
P129.G76 2011
418--dc22
2011001362

ISBN: 978-0-415-56641-4 (hbk)
ISBN: 978-0-415-56642-1 (pbk)
ISBN: 978-0-203-80895-5 (ebk)

Typeset in Joanna
by Saxon Graphics Ltd, Derby

MIX
Paper from
responsible sources
FSC
www.fsc.org   FSC® C004839   Printed and bound in Great Britain by the MPG Books Group

Dedicated to Carole, Dan, Joe, Lewis, Oscar and Sam

Contents

List of figures

List of tables

List of boxes

Acknowledgements

We would like to thank the many people who have helped with the creation of this book. First and foremost, we thank Nadia Seemungal, our commissioning editor at Routledge, who has been with us every step of the way. We would also like to thank Sophie Jaques, Isabelle Cheng and Emma Hudson at Routledge, and Rob Brown and his team at Saxon Graphics, for their advice and support at various stages during this project. We are also very grateful to the anonymous reviewers who provided insightful feedback on draft versions of our manuscript. We would also like to express our thanks to the following colleagues and students for their useful comments and suggestions: Sue Blackwell, Graham Burton, Bob Holland, Almut Koester, Yasuyo Matsumoto, Beth McElmoyle, Gaby Saldanha, James Turner, Alice Yoo and all the students at the Birmingham summer seminars held in Korea and Japan in August 2010. We are especially grateful to the following people for generously allowing us to refer to their work in this book: Annelie Ädel, Yasuyo Matsumoto, Veronica Ormeno, Glen Poupore, Polly Liyen Tang and Mika Tatsumoto. Finally, we are grateful to Sage Publications for kindly granting us permission to reproduce Figure 5.2.

Abbreviations

AAAL	American Association for Applied Linguistics
AILA	International Association of Applied Linguistics
ALAA	Applied Linguistics Association of Australia
BA	Bachelor of Arts degree
BAAL	British Association for Applied Linguistics
BoE	Bank of English
BNC	British National Corpus
CA	Conversation analysis
CDA	Critical discourse analysis
EAP	English for academic purposes
EFL	English as a foreign language
ELT	English language teaching
ESL	English as a second language
ESP	English for specific purposes
KWIC	Key word in context
L1	First language
L2	Second language
LAD	Language acquisition device
MA	Master of Arts degree
MLA	Modern Language Association
MOLT	Motivation orientation of language teaching
MWU	Multi-word units

PhD	Doctor of Philosophy degree
R	R Project for Statistical Computing
SFG	Systemic-functional grammar
SFL	Systemic-functional linguistics
SIGs	Special interest groups
SLA	Second Language Acquisition
SPSS	Statistics Package for Social Scientists
TBI	Task-based interaction
TEFL	Teaching English as a foreign language
TESL	Teaching English as a second language
TESOL	Teaching English to speakers of other languages
TOEFL	Test of English as a foreign language
TTR	Type/token ratios
VLE	Virtual learning environment

Introduction

Who this book is for

We have written this book primarily for students who have just begun, or who are just about to begin, a university programme in applied linguistics or Teaching English as a Foreign or Second Language (TEFL/TESL). However, we also hope that it will be of interest to the curious layperson. Applied linguistics is a highly accessible field of academic study, and its focus on practical problems, questions and issues in which language plays a central role makes it a subject with a potentially very wide appeal. What kinds of grammar should be taught to students learning a foreign language? Should grammar be taught at all? Do journalists consciously or unconsciously manipulate language in order to present their readers with biased or distorted views of particular news events? Is there a need for an international linguistic human rights policy, and if so, how should such a policy be formulated and enforced? Do bilingual schoolchildren have any advantages or disadvantages compared to their monolingual peers? If you find any of these questions interesting, then we hope you will find this book interesting too.

What this book is for

The aim of this book is to provide you with a concise and accessible introduction to contemporary applied linguistics. Although we will try to give you some sense of the range of topics and themes covered by applied linguistics, we are primarily interested in telling you about the different kinds of activities and processes that are involved in *doing* research in applied linguistics, hence the title of our book. We will use a lot of examples to illustrate what is involved in doing applied linguistics research. We will also talk about what kinds of activities you are likely to find yourself doing as a student of applied linguistics. In other words, if we were writing about cars instead of applied linguistics, we would want our book to feel more like a series of introductory or 'taster' driving lessons, rather than a detailed description of all the different car manufacturers and models currently on the road.

How to use this book

This book is designed to be read from cover to cover, but you may also find it useful to return to specific chapters or sections of the book later on in your studies, in order to refresh your memory about a particular topic area, research method or approach to analysis.

The book is divided into ten main chapters. The first four chapters provide a general introduction to the field of applied linguistics by explaining what kind of subject it is, reviewing some of the major topics that fall within its scope, and identifying some of the ways in which applied linguistics has had a practical impact on the wider world. In the next six chapters we focus in more detail on what is actually involved in *doing* applied linguistics, hence the title of our book. We begin by focusing on the analysis of qualitative data collected via questionnaires, interviews and ethnographic observations. We then shift the focus to how applied linguists collect quantitative data for research purposes, and how they analyse these data using descriptive and inferential statistics. In the last two chapters we look at how and why you might analyse individual texts or large computerised corpora of texts in order to address applied linguistics research questions. By showing you examples of how people have actually 'done' applied linguistics (in Chapters 5–10), we aim to give you a good idea of what applied linguistics research actually involves, so that you will be in a good position to start doing applied linguistics for yourself on your degree programme. This will be particularly useful for those of you who are commencing programmes which feature a lot of 'situated learning' activities from day one, and where assignments involve a lot of 'hands-on' testing of applied linguistic theories on real data, or with real students in real classrooms. The book concludes by offering some general advice on how you can take your studies further.

1

Questions about applied linguistics

Introduction

The aim of this chapter is to provide you with a broad and general outline of applied linguistics as an academic subject area. In so doing, we hope to answer some of the questions that new and prospective students of applied linguistics most frequently ask about the subject. In particular, we will try to provide clear answers to the following questions, which we are often asked by prospective students:

- What is applied linguistics?
- What is the difference between linguistics and applied linguistics?
- What is the difference between applied linguistics and second/foreign language teaching?

We will begin by looking at some of the best-known formal definitions of applied linguistics, before moving on to explain what kind of 'applied' subject applied linguistics is. We will then briefly survey the main topic areas that fall within the scope of contemporary applied linguistics. Finally, we will introduce some of the typical ways in which applied linguists go about investigating these topics.

Official and unofficial definitions

If you have searched for definitions of applied linguistics on the Internet or in reference books, you may have been struck by how similar most of them seem to be. A typical example can be found on the website of the International Association for Applied Linguistics (AILA), the leading professional organisation in the field. According to AILA, applied linguistics is 'an interdisciplinary field of research and practice dealing with practical problems of language and communication'. Turning to printed sources, we find that *Applied Linguistics*, one of the most prestigious academic journals in the field, describes the subject as 'the study of language and language-related problems in specific situations in which people use and learn languages', while the respected *Longman Dictionary of Language Teaching and Applied Linguistics* (Richards *et al.* 2002: 28) defines applied linguistics even more concisely as 'the study of language and linguistics in relation to practical problems.' All of these definitions are neatly encapsulated in perhaps the best-known and most frequently-cited definition of all, originally formulated by the eminent applied linguist Chris Brumfit (1995: 27):

> [applied linguistics is] the theoretical and empirical investigation of real-world problems in which language is a central issue.

Brumfit's definition provides a useful starting point for this book, and in the remainder of this chapter we will discuss the two basic questions that this definition raises but does not answer: what 'real-world problems' are applied linguists interested in, and how do they go about investigating them?

Before moving on to consider these questions in detail, however, we first need to deal with an even more fundamental question about applied linguistics: what kind of 'applied' subject is it?

What is 'applied' about applied linguistics?

Applied subjects in higher education can be divided into two contrasting types. The first type of applied subjects focuses very clearly on the practical applications of a single branch of academic knowledge. Applied mathematics, for example, studies how mathematical theories, concepts and processes can be used to solve practical problems in fields as diverse as engineering, computer science and economics. Similarly, applied geology investigates how academic knowledge produced in the 'pure' scientific field of geology can be exploited in practical areas such as mineral exploration, natural resource management and the construction industry.

The second type of applied subjects have no 'pure' or 'theoretical' equivalents, and focus instead on a single (although often very broad) practical domain. Civil engineering, for example, focuses on problems, questions and issues related to the built environment, while education focuses on problems, questions and issues related to teaching and learning. There is no 'pure civil engineering' or 'theoretical education' against which civil engineering or education as applied subjects can be contrasted. On the contrary, subjects such as these are not branches of any single academic discipline at all, but are entirely interdisciplinary in nature. Civil engineering draws on mathematics, physics, materials science, geography, geology, ecology and business management, among many other fields, without being reducible to any one of them. Likewise, education draws on research in disciplines as diverse as psychology, sociology, philosophy, economics and politics, but still maintains its own distinct identity as an academic subject area, and its own distinctive set of goals.

So, what kind of applied subject is applied linguistics? Although the name 'applied linguistics' suggests that it is an applied subject in the same way that applied mathematics and applied geology are applied subjects, applied linguistics is in reality closer in spirit (if not necessarily in content!) to applied subjects like civil engineering or education. While it is certainly true that many if not most applied linguists see the academic discipline of linguistics as their nearest neighbour and most important source of intellectual inspiration, it is also the case that many applied linguists look to other fields for relevant insights into real-world language problems as well – to biology, cultural studies, economics, education, philosophy, politics, psychology and sociology, among others. There are even applied linguists who do not draw on linguistics at all. Researchers working in 'critical' applied linguistics, for instance, base their work almost entirely on theoretical concepts and frameworks derived from postmodernist critical theory, and regard academic knowledge in linguistics as 'fairly irrelevant' to their concerns (Pennycook 2004: 801).

In summary, although applied linguistics enjoys a strong and productive working relationship with linguistics (as we hope to demonstrate throughout this book), our answer to the question 'what is the difference between linguistics and applied linguistics?' is this: applied linguistics is not a branch of linguistics, or of any other academic discipline, for that matter. It is an academic subject area in its own right, with its own set of concerns, its own academic journals, its own professional associations, its own academic qualifications, and its own professional pathways.

The scope of applied linguistics

We now turn from the question of what kind of subject applied linguistics is, to the question of what topic areas fall within its scope. Unfortunately, establishing the boundaries of applied linguistics is no easy task. Part of the problem here is that applied linguistics is still a comparatively young subject. As such, it is still in the process of forming a distinctive identity of its own. In this sense, applied linguistics can be likened to a volcano that has recently sprung out of the sea. Eventually this volcano will turn into an island with a relatively clear shape, but for the time being it is impossible to predict exactly what that shape will be. Another problem – as we will see in more detail later – is that applied linguists do not always agree about which topic areas do and do not (or should and should not) fall within the boundaries of their field. Some prefer to define applied linguistics in very narrow terms, while others take a much broader view of the subject. Finally, attempts to define the scope of applied linguistics are inevitably hampered by the eclectic and interdisciplinary character of applied linguistics as an academic subject area, as mentioned previously. The boundaries of interdisciplinary subjects are, by their very nature, much harder to describe than are those of more traditional academic disciplines, and it may even be the case that applied linguistics cannot ultimately be clearly defined in terms of its scope at all.

Our own approach to this thorny topic will be to distinguish between three broad areas of academic and professional practice, each of which has a recognisably different status in relation to applied linguistics. The first of the three broad areas to be identified here is that of second language teaching and learning. The status of this area vis-à-vis applied linguistics is completely uncontroversial: language teaching and learning have always been universally recognised as central to the concerns of applied linguistics. Indeed, for many people, applied linguistics is the academic study of second language learning and teaching, and it is perhaps for this reason that the question 'what is the difference between applied linguistics and TEFL?' so frequently arises. When applied linguistics first emerged as a subject area in the second half of the twentieth century, it focused mainly on questions surrounding the learning and teaching of foreign languages, and was aimed squarely at experienced language teachers who wished to do a master's degree for reasons of professional development. Taught programmes in applied linguistics provided courses in curriculum, syllabus and materials design, language teaching methodology and classroom management. Specific attention was usually given to the teaching of the four 'macro' skill areas of speaking, listening, reading and writing, together with courses on pronunciation, language testing, teacher education and (as the field expanded) on language school and project management.

Of course, decisions about what to teach and how to teach it need to be grounded in a strong understanding of what language is and how learners learn it, and it is for this reason that applied linguistics programmes have also always included topics that seem to be indistinguishable from those that you might expect to find on a course of studies in 'mainstream' linguistics. It is very likely, for example, that your programme of studies will include coverage of some (or perhaps even all) of the following subjects: phonology (the study of linguistic sound systems), morphology (the study of word components), grammar (the study of the rules that govern word combinations and inflections), lexis (the study of how the entire word stock of a language is organised), semantics (the study of meaning in language), pragmatics (the study of meaning in context), psycholinguistics (the study of how language is acquired, stored and processed by the mind), sociolinguistics (the study of how language shapes and is shaped by society) and discourse analysis (the study of texts and text-making processes). What distinguishes these topics from their equivalents on theoretical linguistics programmes is that they will always be taught with one eye firmly fixed on their practical relevance and applicability.

While the traditional roster of topics listed above continues to be regarded as part of the core content of applied linguistics, the subject has expanded to incorporate a much wider range of concerns in recent years, and it is this expanded range of topics that forms the second horizon of applied linguistic inquiry that we will identify here. This 'new horizon' in applied linguistics spans several distinct content areas. The first of these is mainstream education. By 'mainstream' we mean educational contexts which are primarily funded and influenced by the state, rather than the English language teaching (ELT) context, which is rooted in the practices and concerns of teachers working in private language schools or for cultural exchange organisations such as the British Council or the Peace Corps. This research area includes topics such as migrant education, bilingualism and multilingualism and their relation to schooling, and first language literacy education.

As well as encompassing a broader perspective on language and education in formal contexts, applied linguists have also become increasingly interested in a wide range of issues that might loosely be described together as the politics of language. At a micro level, this interest manifests itself in research that aims to diagnose and ameliorate communication problems arising in a wide range of professional and workplace contexts. Researchers in the now burgeoning subfields of workplace communication and intercultural communication are interested in finding out whether the causes of conflict situations of various kinds can be traced to differences in the preferred communication styles of people from different social and cultural groups. If so, this opens up the possibility of improving relations between individuals and groups by providing them with explicit training or education about such linguistic and cultural differences. And at a macro level of analysis, applied linguists have become increasingly involved in the analysis of national and international language planning and language policy issues, in debates around language maintenance and language loss, and in promoting the concept of linguistic human rights.

Issues of justice and equity also inform two other important developments in applied linguistics, forensic linguistics and critical discourse analysis. The former focuses on applications of linguistic knowledge to the legal process, and the latter aims to identify and critique ways in which linguistic choices and language practices are used to manipulate public opinion, to promote the interests of powerful groups in society, and to oppress, disadvantage and discriminate against others.

We will discuss these various topics in more detail in Chapter 2. Here, the important point to note is that this massive expansion of the applied linguistics curriculum has led to a somewhat confused situation, in which some people still understand applied linguistics in the narrow way discussed earlier (i.e. as the academic study of foreign language teaching), while others see it in the broader terms that we have just reviewed above. Similarly, there are MA programmes in applied linguistics that focus exclusively on ELT, whereas at other universities you can do an applied linguistics degree without focusing on ELT at all. It is no doubt in recognition of these divisions and contradictions that the *Longman Dictionary of Language Teaching and Applied Linguistics* cited earlier in this chapter defines applied linguistics in two different ways, as follows:

1. the study of second and foreign language learning and teaching;
2. the study of language and linguistics in relation to practical problems.

(Richards et al. 2002: 28)

Although this double definition is arguably somewhat redundant when viewed from a purely contemporary perspective (the first definition is clearly encompassed by the second one), it remains relevant for the time being because of what it tells us about the history and development of applied linguistics as an academic subject. Applied linguistics has not yet fully emerged from the period of transition indicated by this double definition, and it must be admitted that there are applied linguists who do not agree with broader view, and who argue that it would be better to scale the boundaries of the field back to their original exclusive focus on ELT. However, it is safe to say that the broader view of the field sketched out above is becoming increasingly widely accepted nowadays, and it would not be at all surprising if in a future edition of the *Longman Dictionary* the narrower of the two definitions quoted above were to be quietly dropped.

Before moving on, we need to mention one further horizon in applied linguistics. This furthest horizon consists of subjects that are sometimes listed by textbooks and other reference sources as subdisciplines within applied linguistics, and which certainly address 'real-world problems in which language is a central issue', but which are not usually regarded as subfields of applied linguistics by practitioners in these fields themselves. Some of these fields, such as translation studies, lexicography (the study and practice of dictionary compilation) and stylistics (the study of how linguistic style varies across literary texts and other text types), have what might be called a semi-autonomous relationship with applied linguistics. While researchers in these fields rarely if ever think of themselves as applied linguists, option courses in these fields are sometimes offered on applied linguistics MA programmes, and papers on topics in these subject areas sometimes appear in applied linguistics journals. Others, such as computational linguistics, clinical linguistics and speech therapy, are almost entirely separate and distinct in practice, and are almost always offered by universities as complete courses of study in their own right.

Applied linguistic approaches to language problems

Thus far, we have defined applied linguistics as 'the theoretical and empirical investigation of real-world problems in which language is a central issue' (Brumfit 1995: 27), and surveyed the main problem areas that applied linguistics currently focuses on. Following on from these discussions, the aim of this final section is to consider in fairly general terms how applied linguists go about investigating the problems, questions and issues that interest and concern them.

Let us begin by looking in a little more detail at what it means to 'investigate' a problem in applied linguistics. As with most other academic subject areas, investigations in applied linguistics can take several forms. Let us imagine for a moment that you want to investigate whether standards of English grammar are slipping among school leavers and university graduates, as is currently being claimed in many sections of the Anglophone media throughout the world. Is English really being 'dumbed down' by its users? One way to investigate this question would be to conduct a literature review. This would involve using your university's library catalogue resources to search for previous academic research papers on this question, and to read these papers in order to see whether their combined results present a clear case for agreeing or disagreeing with the 'dumbing down' view. Alternatively, or additionally, you might want to conduct your own empirical research into this issue, by analysing data that you will have collected yourself from learners, teachers and/or other interested parties. Such research may be qualitative (i.e. collected via observations, case studies or interviews), quantitative (i.e. collected via controlled experiments, questionnaires or tests), or based on the manual analysis of individual texts or the computer-assisted analysis of large electronically-stored collections of texts, or corpora. You might also wish to employ a combination of two or more of these methods.

On the other hand, you might prefer to address this problem at a theoretical level, by examining and critiquing the ideas and assumptions that underpin it. You could, for instance, argue that the whole debate about whether standards of grammar are slipping or not is fundamentally misconceived. This is precisely the line taken by Australian academic Gunther Kress in an interesting debate with the British journalist and broadcaster John Humphrys, published in *The Guardian* newspaper in 2004.[1] While Humphrys took the traditional (and very traditionalist) line that standards are indeed slipping, and that schools need to spend more time teaching 'standard English grammar', Kress argued against the idea that there is such a thing as 'standard' grammar at all. In his view, what schools need to do is help learners to understand grammar not as a set of rigid rules, but as a flexible system of approximate regularities that varies according to situational context: 'Should you need to write a sign for the greengrocer, ok, use apostrophe's like this. But should you be asked to design a website for a government department, your clients are bound to prefer this.'

Whichever approach you take, your ultimate aim should be to reach some kind of understanding of the problem that you have been investigating. This in turn may lead you on to propose a possible solution to this problem, but solutions must also be tested by argument and experiment, and their relevance and applicability must be discussed and evaluated by practitioners, decision makers and other interested parties.

Finally, it is also important to note that applied linguistics is not just about investigating and offering solutions to already established problems, or critiquing analyses and solutions that have been offered by other commentators. It is also an important part of the applied linguist's remit to go about *creating* problems − or more precisely, to go about identifying problems that have hitherto gone unnoticed. A very good example of this 'problematising' approach to applied linguistic inquiry is the recent work done on what is now known as 'English as a Lingua Franca' (Jenkins and Seidlhofer 2001; Seidlhofer 2005). Given the unique status of English as the default language of international communication, it has been observed that the majority of the communicative interactions that take place in English around the world are between non-native speakers, and not between native and non-native speakers of the language. This has led a number of applied linguists to raise the question of whether it is really appropriate for learners to be taught a version of English that conforms to one of the major native speaker norms, such as American or British English, or whether it might not be better to teach them a version of English that conforms to a different set of phonological and grammatical norms altogether, one that better represents the language as it is actually spoken and written in these 'lingua franca' interactions.

Conclusion

In this chapter we have defined applied linguistics as an academic subject that focuses on the analysis of real-world language problems. We have also made the important point that applied linguistics is an interdisciplinary subject, which draws not only on the academic discipline of linguistics for ideas and inspiration, but also on many other fields of study across the humanities and social sciences. We have seen how the scope of applied linguistics has expanded substantially in recent years, and that this expansion has led to a situation in which there is no universal agreement about which topic areas do and do not fall within its boundaries. Finally, we have briefly considered some of the main ways in which applied linguists go about addressing real-world problems. We suggested that applied linguistics includes both 'problem-solving' and 'problematising' orientations; that is, it welcomes not only researchers who are interested in providing answers, but also researchers who are interested in raising questions. Research and critique are equally important research activities in applied linguistics, and (in our view, at least) the best applied linguistics research is that which combines both.

2

Topics in applied linguistics

Introduction

In this chapter we will look in more detail at some of the most important and enduring topics, questions and themes that applied linguistics has addressed since its inception. Our aim is not to provide comprehensive coverage here; given the small size of this book, that would be impossible anyway. Instead, what we want to do is give you a sense of the range, variety and vitality of the topics that applied linguistics encompasses, and introduce you to some of the issues that you may come across at some point in your own studies. You will find references to key texts covering each of these topics in Appendix 2, where we provide suggestions for further reading.

As we saw in Chapter 1, applied linguistics has undergone a process of rapid and dramatic expansion in recent decades. Where once the subject was focused very narrowly on second language teaching and learning, it is now increasingly regarded as covering a much wider range of theoretical and practical concerns. This is not to say that applied linguistics is now moving away from foreign language teaching and learning, however. On the contrary, second language pedagogy remains by far the largest area of research activity in contemporary applied linguistics, and this is likely to remain the case for the foreseeable future. Accordingly, we will begin by looking at some of the main subfields within this key area of applied linguistic research, before moving on to survey some of the newer and less pedagogically-focused developments that have come to the fore in recent years. Our aim in this chapter is to provide a broad outline of the sorts of topics that applied linguists often focus on. Examples of what applied linguists have actually *achieved* in these different areas are given in Chapter 3, where we look at the impact of applied linguistics.

Language teaching methodology

The traditional focus of researchers in the area of language teaching methodology has been on the relative effectiveness of different ways of teaching reading, writing, listening and speaking in a second or foreign language. Research findings and theoretical developments in this area have led to some radical changes in the way languages are taught. Up until the 1950s, the most common approach to language teaching was through the study of grammar rules, followed by exercises involving translation. Since then, there has been a general move towards the use of methods that attempt to create a more genuine need for communication in the language classroom, thus (in theory, at least) making the learning process more natural. Many of these types of methods come under the umbrella heading of the Communicative Approach to language teaching.

There is ongoing debate about the role of explicit grammar teaching in the language classroom, and this has been a fruitful area for a great deal of applied linguistic research. Although there remain a number of different positions on this question, the general consensus is that language learners do benefit from having their attention drawn to target language structures and patterns, but that the teaching of rigid 'grammar rules' can sometimes do more harm than good as they do not accurately describe the way the language actually works.

Much of the work in the area of Language Teaching Methodology involves classroom research. This research spans two broad traditions. Action research, which is usually qualitative and carried out by researchers who are also practising teachers, involves examining specific aspects of a particular teaching/learning situation in a single period of time, generally with the intent of making modifications to the teaching/learning process that (it is hoped) will lead to discernible improvements in educational outcomes. Experimental research, which is usually quantitative, often involves looking at linguistic features or teaching/learning practices that are recordable or observable, and aims to make general statements about how particular linguistic skills or abilities might best be taught.

In both of these traditions a range of instruments is used to examine and measure factors which influence language learning success, learners' attitudes and beliefs and interaction in the language classroom. An interesting finding from this research area is that, contrary to expectations, language learners do not always learn from corrective feedback in the way one might expect them to. In other words, if a learner makes a mistake and the teacher repeats what they said using the correct form, the learner may not take this information on board immediately, and may well go on to make the same mistake in future. This is due to the fact that language teaching and learning involves much more than straightforward knowledge transfer.

In order to understand the language learning process more deeply, it is important to consider what is already in the learner's mind when they come to class. By gaining insights into the ways in which learners process incoming information, researchers aim to identify ways in which language teaching can be improved. Researchers conduct and draw on relevant research into learner autonomy, language learning styles and strategies, the role of memory and mental schemas, embodied cognition, affective factors, cultural frameworks and differences between the students' mother tongue and the language they are learning in order to make concrete proposals as to how language teachers can use their knowledge of learner cognition to make their teaching more effective.

Syllabus and materials design

Research into syllabus and materials design is another key component of language teaching research. Researchers into syllabus and materials design are interested in the order, and the way, in which learning material should be presented to the learner. Researchers' and teachers' views with respect to this issue usually reflect their own understanding of how languages are learned and how they are structured, and in many cases their views are shaped by the way they themselves were taught. Four widely-used syllabus types are:

- the grammatical/structural syllabus;
- the notional/functional syllabus;

- the lexical syllabus; and
- content-based instruction and the task-based syllabus.

The most popular of these four syllabus types is the grammatical/structural syllabus, where the focus is on the ordering of grammatical structures from the simplest to the most complex. Vocabulary and grammar tend to be treated as separate phenomena and the language presented tends to be somewhat artificial, in order to allow for the systematic introduction of grammar 'rules'. Functional/notional syllabi are those which are ordered according to lists of functions and notions which the syllabus designer deems relevant to learners at a particular level. Functions are the 'communicative purposes' for which language is used and include things such as 'advising' or 'persuading', and notions are the contexts in which these functional communicative acts take place. Lexical syllabi have vocabulary rather than grammar as their organising principle, and are heavily influenced by research on computerized language corpora. Unlike the other three syllabus types, the task-based syllabus emphasizes the successful completion, through interaction and communication between learners, of a variety of tasks which are pre-selected by the teacher or syllabus designer for their suitability in promoting the process of acquisition, or for their relevance to learners' needs, rather than the learning of pre-selected linguistic content. Research in this area has had an increasingly strong influence in recent years on the design of published textbooks and on the content of language teacher-training programmes.

Language testing

Like syllabus and materials design, work in the area of language testing is an important aspect of research into how languages are taught and learned. The focus here is on how a learner's language ability can be assessed. A distinction is generally drawn here between achievement testing (which sets out to establish whether learners have met a set of pre-determined linguistic skills which they were specifically taught in class) and proficiency testing (which sets out to establish whether learners have reached an independent 'level' of the target language, at which they can be expected to perform in a variety of situations). Researchers into language testing are interested in answering questions such as: is language learning ability related to general intelligence or is it something different? Is there a subset of skills that combine to create an underlying 'gift for language learning', for which the more technical term is language aptitude? How do different types of tests (such as dictations, gap-fill tests and oral examinations) measure different types of language ability? And to what extent are these different tests reliable indicators of language ability?

Languages for Specific Purposes

Languages for Specific Purposes (LSP) looks at the features of different types of language with a view to teaching learners who are going to have to use these specific types of language in their everyday lives. The groups of people who use specific types of language for a common purpose are sometimes referred to as discourse communities, and the aim of researchers in the area of LSP is to investigate how teachers can best help students to enter these communities.

A major sub-branch of LSP is English for Academic Purposes (EAP), whose main aim is to help prepare international students for study at English-speaking universities. Researchers in this area study the types of language that are used in lectures, seminars and written papers across the range of disciplines that are offered at universities where English is the medium of instruction. They are also interested in studying how the types of language used vary across different disciplines, and across the different spoken and written genres of higher education (e.g. lectures, seminars, research articles, textbooks, argumentative essays, laboratory reports, etc.). They also investigate the effectiveness of different modes of delivery, including for example team teaching with subject lecturers. Related to this is the field of academic literacy. The focus here is more on native speakers of the language who for one reason or another may not be familiar with the linguistic conventions that are common in academic discourse. Again the focus is on describing and teaching or critiquing these conventions in order to enhance student learning levels in higher education.

Another major branch of ESP, Business English, endeavours to describe the major business genres (business correspondence, meetings, negotiations) as well as dealing with the topic of intercultural communication, which is of central importance in the business world.

Work in this area feeds into the development of Business English textbooks and business training courses. ESP research also overlaps with the subfield of workplace communication. Among other things, research in this area has led to the production of training materials for healthcare professionals who work in linguistically diverse communities (see, for example, Roberts *et al.* 2004).

Second Language Acquisition

Researchers in the area of Second Language Acquisition (SLA) are interested in questions such as: is there a natural order of acquisition that remains constant across all language learning situations? To what extent does the acquisition of a second language resemble that of a first language? How is language organised in the mind of a person who speaks more than one language? How does exposure to the target language translate into intake and learning? Traditionally, researchers working in this area have tended to distinguish between learning, which is a conscious process that usually takes place in a classroom, and acquisition, which is a less conscious process that normally takes place outside the classroom (for example when immigrants learn the language of their destination country simply by living there). However the distinction between these two processes quickly becomes problematic as soon as we start to look at authentic language learning situations, which usually involve a combination of conscious and unconscious learning mechanisms. Indeed, recent research suggests that such simple dichotomies do not accurately reflect the process of second language acquisition at all, and that it may be better to conceptualise this process as a 'complex system', drawing on theoretical notions of complexity that are now increasingly commonplace in many other academic fields.

Within the field of Second Language Acquisition researchers who look at bilingualism (or even multilingualism) are interested in the ways in which children born into multilingual families or communities develop an ability to speak more than one language. Given that the majority of the world's population is at least bilingual, this is no small endeavour. They are interested in the ways in which the different languages interact in the brain, how bilingual people switch between their different languages in different situations, and how bilingualism is best fostered. An interesting observation that has been made by researchers working in this area is that people who can already speak more than one language well tend to have some cognitive advantages (for instance greater cognitive flexibility) compared to people who only speak one language, and they find it much easier to learn subsequent languages.

As SLA researchers are interested in studying what goes on in the minds of people who are using and/or learning second languages, they often draw on research in the area of psycholinguistics, which explores the relationship between language and the mind. Psycholinguists look at how language is stored and accessed and at how we derive meaning from the language to which we are exposed. A sub-branch of psycholinguistics called neurolinguistics focuses on the brain itself and looks at the neurological processes underlying the use of language. Psycholinguists are also interested in language impairments and the development of language ability in children. Psycholinguistic research seeks to explain why it is that during spoken and written communication people tend to hear and read what they expected to hear and read, rather than what was *actually* said or written. It also seeks to explain why slips of the tongue occur and why people tend to find it much harder to learn languages as they get older.

Language policy and planning

This subfield of applied linguistics looks at the way language is controlled at international, national and local levels. At the international level it looks at the spread of English around the world and analyses the socio-economic and political causes and consequences of this. At the national level it looks at the role of official languages in maintaining national identity and explores the relationship between official and minority languages. Researchers are interested in issues such as whether immigrants should be forced to speak the same language as the indigenous population, and whether schools should deliver lessons in more than one language. The fact that countries such as Canada or Switzerland are bilingual or even multilingual is in part due to language policy and planning. In other countries minority languages are more likely to be suppressed because of the language policies of the ruling party. At a more local level, the focus might be on the ways in which power relations are established and maintained within an organisation through the use of language. A key concept to emerge from this research is that of linguistic human rights. Some applied linguists have become powerful advocates of the linguistic human rights of minority language speakers in many countries, and have been increasingly successful in raising public awareness of these issues at local, national and international levels.

Forensic linguistics

Forensic linguistics studies the relationship between language and the law. Forensic linguists look at how language is used in the legal process, focusing on the discourse of the police, lawyers, judges and legal documents, and courtroom interaction. Under its narrower definition, forensic linguistics refers to the examination of linguistic evidence in court. It is used in cases of disputed authorship of written texts (such as police statements) and where there are issues of plagiarism. Forensic linguists provide information that helps jurors decide whether a particular person is likely to have been the author of a particular text. They also study cases where inaccurate translations of statements made by non-native speakers have led to miscarriages of justice, and are therefore able to advise on the treatment of people (such as children, non-native speakers or people with learning difficulties) who may have difficulties with – and thus potentially be disadvantaged by – the language of the legal system.

Sociolinguistics and critical discourse analysis

Sociolinguistics looks at the relationship between language and society. The focus is on variation in the way people use language as well as on language change. Researchers in this area are interested in how people use language to create and maintain social structures and hierarchies. They also look at the role of language in creating and maintaining a person's identity. The language one speaks, the accent one has, the ways in which people change their accent (or even their language) when speaking to different people in different social situations all come under the microscope of the sociolinguist.

One of the key findings to emerge from research in sociolinguistics is that variables such as accent, dialect and gender are intimately bound up with social inequalities and injustices of various kinds. For example, sociolinguists have shown that speakers who have certain regional accents are less likely to be successful at job interviews than are speakers of more prestigious dialectal variants. Similarly, research on gender and language has shown how girls and boys are socialised from a very early age into talking in ways that are deemed 'correct' for their gender identity, and sanctioned in various ways if they transgress these implicit linguistic boundaries. Taking such observations as its starting point, critical discourse analysis (CDA) has developed into a distinct branch of applied linguistic research that adopts an explicitly political stance towards the analysis of the relationship between language and society. For practitioners of CDA, it is not enough simply to describe or diagnose the linguistic determinants of social inequality; rather, the CDA agenda is one that aims to ameliorate social inequality and promote social justice. This is usually done by combining linguistic analysis with theoretical insights drawn from sociology and cultural studies in order to identify and critique the ideologies that, it is argued, lie behind individual texts. Much of the focus in CDA since its inception has been on the mass media; researchers working in this area have sought to uncover the underlying rhetorical objectives and ideological positions reflected in news coverage of public events, thereby showing how powerful groups in society attempt to manipulate public opinion. More recent work has broadened this perspective somewhat, to include analyses of everyday language that – often unwittingly – promotes discrimination against minority groups in society.

Translation studies

Language policy and planning, forensic linguistics and CDA are all areas of research that have been developed largely or entirely within applied linguistics. But lists of topics that are deemed to fall under the general rubric of applied linguistics often include subjects that either predate it or are semi-autonomous from it. One of the most frequently cited of these more loosely affiliated fields is translation studies. Researchers in translation studies study the choices that people make when translating from one language to another. There is often a trade-off between achieving loyalty to the original text and achieving naturalness in the target language, and translators will make choices depending on the target audience of the translated document, as well as for their own personal or ideological reasons. For example, in an English text, a writer might refer to someone as their 'right hand man'. If this expression does not exist in the language that the text is being translated into, the translator may find an alternative corresponding expression, or they may try to retain authenticity by translating it directly, or if they have strong feminist sentiments, they may opt to change the wording to 'person'. Translation studies researchers look at these types of choices in an attempt to access the thought processes that take place in the mind of the translator while he or she is translating.

Translation studies scholars are also interested in studying the impact that translations or collections of translations have had in the socio-cultural situation of the languages involved. They attempt to use existing theories of translation to predict what the process of translation is likely to involve for particular pairs of languages and types of text. This work has applications in translator training, the preparation of translation aids, such as dictionaries, grammars, term banks and in recent years, automatic translators, the establishment of translation policy (which involves giving advice on the role of the translator in a given socio-cultural context, deciding on the economic position of the translator, deciding which texts need to be translated, or deciding what role translation should play in the teaching of foreign languages), and translation criticism, which concerns itself with the development of criteria for the evaluation of the quality or effectiveness of the translation product.

Lexicography

Another specialist field that enjoys a 'semi-autonomous' relationship with applied linguistics is lexicography. Lexicography is the practice of compiling dictionaries, and lexicographers are the specialist authors who carry out the process of dictionary compilation. In applied linguistics, however, the field of lexicography is also understood as including investigations of the decisions that lexicographers make when compiling dictionaries, and on the look-up strategies that dictionary users deploy when consulting them. Recent debates in this field have focused on the relative merits of traditional and full-sentence definition styles, and on how the different senses of polysemous words (i.e. words with multiple meanings) should be ordered in learners' dictionaries. For example, some lexicographers argue that the word 'back' should be presented as an adverb (as in *go back, lean back,* or *back home*) before it is presented as a noun describing a part of the human body, on the grounds that the adverbial usage is much more frequent in native speaker usage. Other lexicographers argue for the opposite policy, on the grounds that the literal meaning expressed by the noun is the basic or 'prototypical' meaning from which all the non-literal adverbial meanings of 'back' are derived.

Linguistics and applied linguistics

One question that may still be in your mind after having read about all these topics, is the following: what exactly is the relationship between 'applied' linguistics and 'pure' or 'mainstream' linguistics? As we suggested in Chapter 1, it would be a mistake to assume that applied linguistics is nothing more than some kind of ancillary branch of linguistics, which simply takes ideas from mainstream theoretical or descriptive linguistics and applies them to a range of practical problems. While it is certainly true that applied linguistics draws extensively on research and theory originally developed in 'mainstream' linguistics, it is equally important to emphasize that applied linguistics goes well beyond the scope of 'mainstream' linguistics in its endeavour to address real-world issues. In doing so, it has contributed a number of important new perspectives back into linguistic research and theory. For reasons of space, we will restrict ourselves to just one set of illustrative examples here, by considering some of the contributions that applied linguistics has made to one of the most ostensibly abstract and theoretical of all of the subfields within linguistics: grammatical theory.

Grammar has of course always been a core topic within the discipline of linguistics, but since the late 1950s the field has come to be dominated by grammatical theory to an unprecedented extent. Overwhelmingly, the grammatical theory that has established itself as the de facto standard approach in linguistics is Noam Chomsky's generative grammar. Generative grammar is concerned with the identification of rules that allow native speakers of a language to distinguish grammatical sentences in a language from ungrammatical ones. In this approach, syntax (i.e. the set of rules governing word order) is regarded as largely independent of semantics (i.e. the meanings expressed by words). For example, Chomsky coined the famous sentence 'colourless green ideas sleep furiously' in order to demonstrate that it is possible for a sentence to be syntactically 'correct' (and to be perceived as such by native speakers) without being in any way meaningful. Chomsky and his followers use people's intuitive knowledge of syntactic correctness to argue that there are certain aspects of grammar that are universal, that is, common to all human languages (such as the fact that there are relationships between words) and others that vary from one language to the next (for example, the fact that there are certain situations where a definite article is required in some languages but not others). These and other observations have led Chomsky to propose that we are all equipped with an independent Language Acquisition Device (LAD) in our minds, which is responsible for language acquisition and processing, and which is independent from other types of cognitive processing.

Applied linguists have responded to generative grammar in a variety of ways. In fields such as SLA, many researchers have not only adopted the generative grammar approach, but have also taken it in an entirely new direction, by asking whether and to what extent learners of second languages also have access to the same Language Acquisition Device that (according to generativist theory) governs the process of first language acquisition. Essentially, there are three different positions on this issue. Some researchers have argued that the LAD is fully operational in second language learning, and cite empirical studies showing that adult learners of English as a second language can master features of English that simply do not exist in their first language (L1). Others argue that access to the LAD is possible to some degree, but will always be mediated (and sometimes hindered) by what speakers subconsciously know about their first language. Finally, there are researchers who propose that there is a critical period (roughly at the age of puberty) beyond which learners of second languages no longer have access to the LAD at all. Researchers who take this view have pointed to the often striking differences in the final second language proficiency attainment levels of immigrant children and their parents as evidence in support of this 'no second language' view.

Because it separates syntax from semantics and pragmatics, and regards linguistic theory as essentially concerned with psychological questions, generative grammar has found less favour among applied linguists who believe that there is a relationship between grammar and meaning, and who are more interested in social problems than psychological processes. These researchers have tended to work with alternative approaches to grammatical theory. By far the most popular of these over the last two decades has been systemic-functional grammar (SFG). Developed by the linguist Michael Halliday, SFG attempts to provide an account of the grammar of the language as it is used in actual social situations, and places meaning, or what Halliday terms 'function', at the centre of its theoretical model. Systemic-functional grammarians study the communicative and rhetorical purposes of language, and consider the grammatical resources that a language makes available to the speaker or writer in a given communicative context. A basic tenet of SFG is that any text, whether written or spoken, conveys three kinds of meaning. First, it conveys ideas (this is its field). Second, it sets up some sort of relationship with the reader or listener (this is its tenor) and third, it is delivered in a particular form, such as a letter or a talk (this is its mode).

Because it brings meaning to the forefront of grammatical description, SFG has been used extensively by researchers and teachers involved in language and literacy education, most notably in Australia, where it formed the theoretical basis for a major project that aimed to improve literacy standards in socially disadvantaged schools. Crucially, the experience of applying SFG framework in this 'Disadvantaged Schools Project' led the researchers involved in it to develop a new branch of systemic-functional linguistics called appraisal theory, as they noticed that SFG lacked a detailed framework for modelling the lexical and grammatical resources for expressing evaluative meanings in texts.

Another approach whose increasing popularity owes much to applied linguistics is cognitive grammar. Like SFG, cognitive grammar has meaning (i.e. semantics) at its core and argues that it is inseparable from syntax. Unlike SFG, which sees language as a social phenomenon, cognitive grammar is primarily interested in psychological processes that occur within the minds of individual speakers as they interact with the physical world around them. According to cognitive grammarians, there is no autonomous, special-purpose language acquisition device that is responsible for language acquisition and language processing. They argue that a single set of cognitive processes operates across all areas of language, and that these processes are involved in other types of knowledge and learning besides language. The centrality of meaning is thus a fundamental claim of cognitive grammarians. When new words and phrases enter a language, they tend to do so as 'content' words, which means that they have concrete, lexical meanings. Over time, through the process of grammaticalisation, some of these words and phrases become 'function' words; that is to say, they acquire more schematic, grammatical meanings which are different from, yet related to, their original lexical meaning. For example, the original meaning of 'going to' in English refers to movement and travel. However, over time, this phrase has acquired a much more common *grammatical* meaning as an indicator of future action.

Both cognitive grammar and SFG emphasise the fact that linguistic meaning typically operates at the level of the phrase rather than the individual word. This idea is given even more prominence in the third grammatical theory that we want to introduce here pattern grammar. Pattern grammar is an approach to grammar derived from corpus linguistics, the computer-assisted analysis of multi-million-word databases (or 'corpora') of authentic language data. (We will discuss corpus linguistics in detail in Chapter 10.) The basic idea of pattern grammar is that most linguistic meanings reside neither in individual words nor in the structures in which they appear, but in the combination of the two. To illustrate this, consider the following two sentences:

(a) It's possible that she didn't get the message.

(b) It's possible to leave a message.

As you can see, although the adjective *possible* occurs in both sentences, it means something very different in each case. Specifically, sentence (a) can be paraphrased as '*Maybe* she didn't get the message', while a suitable paraphrase for sentence (b) would be something like '*You can* leave a message'. Such observations have led pattern grammarians to propose that it makes no sense to ask what *possible* means – indeed, from a pattern grammar perspective, the word-form *possible* does not mean anything at all itself. Rather, pattern grammarians argue that the 'maybe' and 'you can' meanings in sentences (a) and (b) above are a property of the combinations *possible + that-clause* and *possible + to-infinitive clause* respectively.

Pattern grammar is in many respects very similar to another approach to grammar that is now very popular in cognitive linguistics: construction grammar. Two of the main differences between the two approaches are that pattern grammar is based entirely on empirical observations derived from corpus data, whereas construction grammar tends not to be, and that construction grammar describes relationships between different constructions (or patterns) whereas pattern grammar tends not to focus on such relationships. From the point of view of the current discussion, the most important point to note is that although pattern grammar was originally developed within a very clearly applied linguistic framework, it is now seen (together with construction grammar) as offering an increasingly persuasive critique of, and challenge to, the generativist orthodoxy within mainstream theoretical linguistics.

Conclusion

This chapter has introduced you to some of the many topics that you might encounter as a student of applied linguistics. We have looked in particular at the subfields of language teaching methodology, syllabus and materials design, language testing, languages for specific purposes, second language acquisition, language policy and planning, forensic linguistics, sociolinguistics and Critical Discourse Analysis, translation studies and lexicography. We have also revisited and expanded upon the question (initially raised in Chapter 1) of how applied linguistics relates to mainstream theoretical linguistics. Here, we saw that applied linguistics is not parasitic on linguistic theory, but engages actively with it in a variety of ways: by extending it (as in the example of the Language Acquisition Device and L2 acquisition); by developing alternatives to it (as in the case of systemic-functional grammar); and by directly challenging dominant ideas within it (as in the case of cognitive grammar and pattern grammar).

3

The impact of applied linguistics

Introduction

In Chapter 2 we looked at the kinds of topics that applied linguists are interested in and at the kinds of research questions they set themselves. In this chapter we go into more depth, describing in detail a number of real-world studies where applied linguistic research has had an impact on the wider world. We start by looking at work in applied linguistics that has influenced both the ways in which languages are taught and the types of language that learners are exposed to. From this, we then broaden our approach to look at how research in applied linguistics has led to a better understanding of different types of discourse, outlining a number of studies whose findings have helped people to engage with or become members of particular social and cultural groups. Finally we turn to a particularly important area to which linguistics has been applied: the legal system. We discuss cases where the work of linguists has helped send the guilty to prison as well as prove innocence. We close the chapter by examining the important contribution that applied linguistics has made to cross-cultural understanding, and discuss studies whose findings have had particular relevance for people involved in international business communication. The overall aim of the chapter is to cover a range of different types of research studies that have been conducted in the area and to evaluate the impact that they have had on the world beyond applied linguistics. This will prepare the ground for the remainder of this book, in which we will look in more detail at the practicalities of how applied linguistics research projects such as these are actually carried out.

How applied linguistics has influenced second language teaching

Work in applied linguistics has had a significant impact on the way in which second and foreign languages are taught. Work in language teaching has followed two interrelated strands. The first looks at how language should be taught, the focus here being on how language is best presented to learners and what kinds of activities are most conducive to language learning. The second focuses more on what kind of language should be taught. Recent studies have revealed that spoken language has its own grammar which differs in places from the grammar of the written language (Carter and McCarthy 2006). Traditionally the grammar components of language classes have tended to focus on written grammar, but the advent of spoken corpora has revealed patterns in spoken language that could usefully be taught to language learners. We will look at some of these in the next section. We begin, however, by looking at how applied linguistic research has affected the ways in which languages are taught.

The impact of applied linguistic research on the teaching of languages has been substantial. Its main manifestation has been in the form of an increased focus on communication and meaning, which has led to more communicative approaches to language teaching. The key tenets of communicative approaches to language learning and teaching are that learning a language is about learning to communicate, and that learning can actually take place through communication. In other words:

- Learners learn a language through using it to communicate
- Authentic and meaningful communication is the goal of classroom activities
- Fluency is an important part of communication
- Communication involves the integration of different language skills
- Learning is a process of creative construction and involves trial and error

(Richards and Rodgers 2001: 172)

For many people, the beginning of the communicative movement is marked by H.G. Widdowson's *Teaching Lange as Communication* (published in 1978), and by Brumfit and Johnson's (1979) book *The Communicative Approach to Language Learning*, which argued that language learning should not just be about learning grammar rules and vocabulary, but should focus on teaching learners how to use the language that they have learned to express themselves effectively, and to understand how linguistic meanings relate to the social and situational contexts in which they occur. That language teaching up until this point was not in any way 'communicative' in this sense is of course an overstatement, but it is fair to say that this period marked the beginning of a systematic examination of what it means to 'communicate' in a foreign language, and of what language learners need to learn if they are to 'communicate' effectively.

Communicative approaches to language teaching thus differ from previous approaches to language learning in that they are competency based. That is to say, they tend to focus on the outcomes of learning. They look at what learners might be expected to do with the language, and use these to inform the ways in which the language is taught. Ultimately, then, the goal of communicative language teaching is to foster 'the ability not only to apply the grammatical rules of a language in order to form grammatically correct sentences but also to know when and where to use these sentences and to whom' (Richards *et al*. 1992: 65).

In order for this definition to be useful to language teachers, it is important to break it down into a set of subskills. Various suggestions have been made as to how this can be done (see, for example, Canale and Swain 1980; Bachman 1990) but one of the most encompassing taxonomies is proposed by Hedge (2000). Hedge divides communicative competence into five components: linguistic competence; pragmatic competence; discourse competence; strategic competence; and fluency.

Linguistic competence refers to one's knowledge of the language itself, and includes knowledge of vocabulary, morphology, syntax and phonology (the 'nuts and bolts' of language) as well as knowledge about how the different parts of a text fit together and are generally organised. It is important to remember that linguistic competence is indeed a component of communicative competence, and that it is incorrect to say that communicative language teaching is all about 'communication', and that it therefore does not involve grammar teaching. In fact the teaching of grammar should be an important component of communicative approaches to language teaching.

Pragmatic competence is slightly more difficult to explain. If I spotted a cake on the table at a friend's house and said to my friend, 'Wow, that cake looks good', it could be that I am angling for a piece of it, or it could be that I am simply admiring it, or it could even be that I am being sarcastic. The context, including the relationship that I have with my friend would be of central importance in determining the actual meaning, that is to say, the illocutionary force of my utterance. To give another example, if someone were to ring up their partner and say 'I'm standing right outside the fish and chip shop and it smells fantastic – I was wondering if you'd put the dinner on yet', this might reasonably be inferred to mean 'Would you like me to buy us some fish and chips for dinner?' And if someone asks 'Have we got any biscuits left?' and receives the reply 'I don't know, but Joe was on his own in the kitchen for a very long time yesterday evening', he or she may well infer that Joe has eaten all the biscuits, so there probably aren't any left. In each of these examples, the skill of the interpreter lies in identifying the appropriate form-function relationship.

One form can have many different functions, depending on the context, and one function can be expressed through a variety of different forms, depending on the formality of the situation: 'Would you mind not treading on my toe' can perform the same function (in British English, at least) as 'Ouch that hurts, get off!' so being able to use expressions that convey the right register and level of formality is important. In Hedge's words, displaying pragmatic competence in language production involves knowing 'what is appropriate, what is incongruous, and what might cause offence' (2000: 50). In other words, pragmatic competence refers to one's ability to understand the message behind the words that we read or hear, or to make clear one's own message through careful use of words. It is what (usually) prevents us from misunderstanding one another. Up until the advent of communicative approaches to language teaching, there had been little explicit focus on the relationship between form and function, or on how knowledge of this relationship can be taught to language learners. Early attempts to incorporate it into materials resulted in so-called 'functional' syllabi where a function, such as 'requesting' was identified and a list of expressions that could be used to perform that function was presented to the students. More recent approaches have emphasized the fact that pragmatic competence does not develop automatically with linguistic competence, and that it is more closely related to motivation and the extent to which a learner identifies with the target language community (Kasper and Roever 2005). The explicit explanation of indirect speech acts, presented in context, appears to be the most effective way of teaching them.

Discourse competence refers to those abilities that are required to create and understand coherent written and spoken discourse. It is perhaps most useful to think of these rules in terms of cohesion (i.e. lexical and grammatical links) and coherence (i.e. appropriate combination of groups of utterances in terms of their communicative function). Both cohesion and coherence refer to the ways in which words and ideas are linked in a text. Discourse competence applies not only to references to other parts of the text but also to things outside the text. There is also a need to understand ellipsis (the omission of gramatically non-essential words, phrases and clauses) and to grasp a speaker's intentions when very little information is actually provided in the exact words used by the speaker.

Strategic competence, according to Canale and Swain, 'is made up of verbal and non-verbal communication strategies that may be called into action to compensate for breakdowns in communication due to performance variables or to insufficient competence' (1980: 30). So if for example, you don't know the word 'chess board' you might say something like: 'It's a game. There is a square. It's got black and white squares, and small figures move around on it'. Canale and Swain divide communication strategies into two types: those that compensate for lack of knowledge of grammatical forms, and those that compensate for lack of sociolinguistic knowledge. There is some debate over whether it is useful to train students in the use of communication strategies, as it may actually make them lazy in their use of the target language! In other words, if they can always rely on avoidance strategies such as circumlocution and mime, there is less of a need for them to actually learn any new vocabulary or grammar. Skehan (1998) argues that this will lead to fossilisation, a phenomenon whereby language learners seem to stop improving once they have achieved a certain level of communicative competence. Others argue that the use of communication strategies is always good as it keeps the conversation going, allowing for more input which in turn will lead to more learning. Some studies have shown that training students explicitly in the use of communication strategies can make them appear more communicatively competent in oral examinations (Nakatani 2005) but the extent to which the use of such strategies leads to fossilisation is as yet unexplored, so Skehan's concerns are not without foundation.

Related to strategic competence is the last component of communicative competence, namely fluency. As Hedge points out, fluency is a broad term, and is concerned with the linking together of ideas, words and sounds in a way which enables learners to communicate 'without inappropriate slowness or undue hesitation' (2000: 54). More recently, Carter and McCarthy (2006) have begun to use the more encompassing term 'confluence' which refers to a speaker's ability to keep the conversation going, hold the floor, understand what's being said to them and respond to it appropriately. In many ways 'confluence' is a more useful term than 'fluency' as it does away with the somewhat artificial distinction between 'rates of speech' and interactive spoken communication.

So what effects has this focus on communicative competence had on the way languages are actually taught? In language teaching circles there has been much debate about how communicative language teaching methodologies can best be implemented in the language classroom. This has led to an increased popularity of teaching methods such as task-based learning. This involves the use of tasks where the focus is primarily on meaning, and work on form follows. There are different ways of defining a 'task' but one of the most comprehensive definitions is that proposed by Nunan (2004: 4):

> a piece of classroom work that involves learners in comprehending, manipulating, producing or interacting in the target language while their attention is focused on mobilizing their grammatical knowledge in order to express meaning, and in which the intention is to convey meaning rather than to manipulate form. The task should also have a sense of completeness, being able to stand alone as a communicative act in its own right with a beginning, a middle and an end.

Many textbooks, particularly those published in the area of English language teaching, now have a predominantly communicative focus, and elements of task-based learning can be found in a wide variety of course books and language teaching syllabi worldwide. However, this is not to say that the change has been universal. There are many places where, for very good local reasons, communicative approaches to language teaching have not been adopted. What applied linguistics has done is to raise the issue of communicative competence and define it in a way that is useful to language educators. Whether or not they act on this information remains, in many cases, a matter of choice although there are some countries (for example Japan) where communicative language teaching has become part of a national, government-led, language teaching policy, at least on an official level. Also, in Australia, systemic-functional linguistics (introduced in Chapter 2) has been heavily influential on government policy for the teaching of English to immigrants. This approach places a strong emphasis on the analysis of form-function relationships, and thus prioritises what Hedge would call pragmatic competence.

How exactly do applied linguists go about making the sorts of discoveries that have been mentioned in this section? Although 'communicative language ability' and 'communicative competence' began life as theoretical constructs there has since been a great deal of work investigating the nature of the competences that need to be acquired in different contexts, and on the most effective ways of fostering these competencies in language learners. Some of this work has involved discourse analysis; this will be discussed in more detail in Chapter 9. Other work has involved empirical studies designed to investigate the relative effectiveness of different language teaching approaches that focus on different degrees and aspects of communicative competence. This has involved a mixture of different types of research including quantitative approaches, where the outcomes of different language teaching techniques are compared in terms of the impact they have on the language learned by the students, and more qualitative approaches, involving classroom observation and interviews, which have attempted to ascertain, for example, how the different language teaching approaches affect classroom dynamics and student motivation. Examples showing how such studies are conducted are given in Chapters 5 to 8.

How applied linguistics has influenced the types of language that learners are exposed to

Applied linguistic research has led to an increased awareness of the fact that language change is a normal part of human life and that it does not necessarily constitute a 'fall in standards'. A good example of this can be seen in the recent work of applied linguists Ronald Carter and Michael McCarthy on the grammar of spoken English. Carter and McCarthy (2006) outline a number of key characteristics of spoken English in their highly acclaimed corpus-based reference grammar of English. They (and others) suggest that spoken English grammar is characterised by:

- the use of the active voice; the frequent use of 'topic-comment' structures, where the speaker mentions the thing he or she is interested in first, then tells us what he or she wants to say about it, as in: 'You know Kevin, the guy we saw yesterday, I think he quite likes you ...';
- a lack of explicit logical connectors, such as 'therefore', 'because', 'so'; frequent references to things outside the text;
- ellipsis;
- low levels of grammatical subordination;
- the use of pauses and fillers; and
- the use of vague and idiomatic language.

In terms of sentence structure, spoken English tends to be characterized by the presence of modifiers after, rather than before the noun, so whereas in written (British) English one might write: 'it's a big, six-bedroom house' in spoken (British) English one might be more likely to say 'yeah, it's a big house, six bedrooms (ibid.: 169). Subordination is expressed differently in spoken and written English. For example, let us look at the following citation from Carter and McCarthy's corpus:

> You saying about that chap with the newspaper, that, one of dad's many stories of how he escaped death during his long life was one ...

Here the opening phrase 'You saying about that chap with the newspaper' provides the context for what is about to be said. As such, it functions as a subordinate clause, but it is not marked as such. The 'topic-comment' structure is shown in the following examples:

> Madge, one of the secretaries at work, her daughter got married last week.

> My friend, Janet, her sister has just emigrated to Brazil.

Here, the topic is foregrounded and what the speaker has to say about it comes next. This sentence pattern tends not to be found in written

English; indeed, it would be criticised by many people as being ungrammatical if they encountered it in a written text (unless it was part of a naturalistic spoken dialogue in a novel or a play).

Tails are also common in spoken English. These are typically noun phrases that are used to clarify something that has gone before:

They're incredibly nice, our neighbours.

Are they both at university, your brother's kids?

Another characteristic feature of spoken English is that in interrogatives, the initial auxiliary verb is often missing:

You been eating biscuits again?

The dog bothering you?

McCarthy and Carter comment that whereas subject and verb ellipsis are regarded as minor features of written grammar, they are of central importance in spoken grammar. Such ellipsis is particularly common in fixed phrases, such as 'sounds good', 'absolutely right', and 'good job'.

Vague language is particularly prominent in spoken English and often serves particular functions such as relationship building, mitigation and appeals to shared knowledge, as we can see in the following examples:

I've been working hard and travelling all the time and all that sort of thing

They can easily be knocked over and things

The phrases 'all that sort of thing' and 'and things' are intelligible to the listener insofar as they gesture to shared knowledge about the hardships associated with work and travel in the first example, and about the properties of delicate and unstable objects on the other.

These are just some of the examples that Carter and McCarthy provide of the features of spoken English. In English language teaching classrooms and textbooks there is an increasing awareness of these language forms and of their importance in spoken English. There are now specific textbooks designed to introduce learners to the features of spoken

English. These include Carter and McCarthy's *Exploring Spoken English* (1997), which contains extracts of authentic conversations recorded in the United Kingdom. These extracts are followed by exercises and commentaries that teachers and learners can use together, to explore the features of spoken British English in depth.

Increasingly, applied linguists have turned their attention to different types of non-traditional discourse and have made these an explicit subject of study. For example, Tagg (2009) investigated the language used in text messaging. This language was found to be highly creative, pushing at the frontiers of language change but following many of the rules according to which languages normally evolve. The message that comes from work such as this is that language change is a natural, healthy process, reflecting changes in society, and does not necessarily constitute 'language decay', as some media commentators would have us believe.

A particularly important contribution of applied linguistics to the field of language learning has been the contribution of corpus linguistics to the ways learner dictionaries are written. The advent of electronic language corpora revolutionised the way dictionaries, particularly learner dictionaries, are compiled. Up until the early 1980s, most dictionary work was based on introspection, but researchers involved in the University of Birmingham/ HarperCollins COBUILD dictionary project began to use real language data to compile the first corpus-based learners' dictionary. Using computers to analyse large quantities of electronically stored language data, lexicographers were able to work out how frequent certain senses of words are, and what types of phrases they tend to be found in, rather than relying on their own intuitions. The information that corpus-based dictionaries contain is therefore of much more practical benefit to learners than the sort of information that could be found in more traditional dictionaries. Although corpus-based approaches to dictionary compilation began in the area of learners' dictionaries, they have now spread to all types of dictionaries and have entered the mainstream, and it would now be very unusual nowadays for a dictionary to be compiled without the use of a corpus.

How applied linguistics has led to a better understanding of different types of discourse

Strongly related to the language description work we have just seen is the area of applied linguistic research that investigates the features of different types of discourse. Groups of people who use specific types of language for a common purpose are sometimes referred to as discourse communities, and the language spoken by these discourse communities often has its own unique features. In order to fully understand these communities, or to become a member oneself, it is useful to be aware of the characteristics of the particular language features used when producing or participating in genres that are typical of those communities. For example, genres that are popular among the discourse communities of academics include formal lectures, informal seminars and academic articles. Some analysts attempt to identify the features of different genres so that these features can then be taught to people who will at some point need to use them in their daily lives. One of the most famous examples of genre analysis is that carried out by John Swales (1990), who studied the features of academic articles in which research results are reported. He found that the introductions to such articles often follow the same pattern, he describes in terms of four 'moves':

Move 1   Establish the research field, asserting briefly how significant, relevant and important one's chosen topic is.

Move 2   Summarize previous research, giving a few key references.

Move 3   Prepare for present research by indicating a gap in the existing knowledge that needs to be filled or by raising a question about previous research.

Move 4   Introduce one's own research, stating the purpose of the research. Outline what one intends to do or what hypothesis will be tested.

Students on courses that are preparing them for study at university, or research students who are being trained to publish, will often have this pattern (or a later version of it, in which Moves 1 and 2 have been merged) pointed out to them so that they can use it to better understand research articles, and to write research articles themselves.

   Genre analysis is also starting to be used to teach other types of writing in schools in a number of countries. For example, in English lessons in UK schools, pupils are encouraged to read and imitate certain genres. In order to help them do so, their teachers will sometimes point out the move structures of those particular genres. For example, when writing stories, children are encouraged to set the scene, introduce the characters, introduce the problem, show how it was resolved, and offer a conclusion. These approaches to writing are a direct result of research in applied linguistics. Care needs to be taken however not to over-apply findings from research in applied linguistics and to become too prescriptive in one's approach to genre. The main thing to bear in mind is that these patterns are what people *tend* to use when using these genres, and that variation from the norm is acceptable. It is however helpful for pupils to know what the 'norm' actually is.

Discourse analysts also investigate how language is used, either consciously or subconsciously, to convey ideology. Findings from this research, which is sometimes referred to as Critical Discourse Analysis, have direct applications in the political arena. One of the most widely-used models of Critical Discourse Analysis is proposed by Fairclough (2003). This model combines a focus on the internal properties of texts (i.e. the uses that they make of grammar, semantics, lexis and phonology) with a focus on their external properties (i.e. the relations that they have with more general social practices). Critical discourse analysts are interested in what speech functions are prominent in the texts, how people and ideas are represented, and what kind of stance or attitude is conveyed. Drawing on this information, they attempt to identify what the writer is trying to do with the text, and how he or she is using the text to represent the world. Fairclough's model assumes that no discourse can be completely neutral, and that a speaker's or writer's language choices convey particular ideologies, even at very microscopic levels. For example, Clark (1992) uses the model to show how the reporting of a rape in *The Sun* newspaper downplays the role of the rapist by putting relevant sentences in the passive voice, thus reducing the agency of the rapist. The examples cited are:

> Two of Steed's rape victims – aged 19 and 20 – had a screwdriver held at their throats as they were forced to submit.

> His third victim, a 39-year-old mother of three, was attacked at gunpoint after Steed forced her car off the M4.

The rapist himself is not clearly present in these examples. At no point do we see sentences in which the rapist is given any agency, such as 'The rapist attacked his victim'. The only case of agency occurs in the second example, where the object is 'the car', not the woman. Clark argues that the choice of words and structures in these examples turns the focus of the reader away from Steed himself and thus downplays his role in the rapes. Other examples that are similar to this include the type of vocabulary that is often used to describe car crashes. For example, people will often say that they 'had an accident' or 'had a crash'. They will rarely admit that they themselves 'drove their car into a tree'.

Discourse analysts have used this and similar approaches to analyse the language of politicians in order to show how they subtly convey their own ideology through their choices of words and word order in their speeches and in writing. They have also used such approaches to show how the writing of academics, scientists and other experts is often not as objective as it is commonly assumed to be. An excellent example of this is Cook (2004), who uses a variety of analytical techniques to challenge the arguments put forward by those who support the introduction of genetically modified (or GM) food crops into agricultural production. Among other things, Cook's analysis shows that the pro-GM lobby makes extensive use of subtle but clearly identifiable 'smear' tactics to discredit the views of its opponents. Cook's book is also noteworthy in that it is deliberately written in such a way that it is accessible to general audiences who have no specialist knowledge or expertise in either applied linguistics or GM science.

A valid objection that is sometimes raised about critical analyses such as these is that they tell us nothing about how ideologically loaded texts are interpreted by listeners or readers. That is, even if the analyst is correct in claiming that a speaker or writer is deliberately employing particular linguistic strategies in an attempt to influence or mislead an audience, it does not follow from this that the audience in question will necessarily be influenced in the way that the speaker or writer intends by such strategies (O'Halloran 2003; Widdowson 2004). In this regard, the work of the Belgian applied linguist Frank Boers and his colleagues is of particular interest. Boers and Demecheleer (1995) studied the ways in which comparable publications in English, Dutch and French talked about economics. They found that in the English publication these issues were more likely to be conceptualised (or 'metaphorically construed', in their terms) as ailments or sporting competitions that need to be won. In the French and Dutch publications these metaphors were much rarer, and the French publication in particular tended to make more use of food metaphors. In a follow-up study using business studies students as his test subjects, Boers (1997) showed that by construing economics in such fundamentally different ways, writers can dramatically influence their readers' views of these issues. When asked how particular economic problems could be resolved, Boers' students recommended very different courses of action depending on how the issue has been construed metaphorically in the texts they had previously been exposed to.

How applied linguistics has influenced life and death decisions: language and the law

Legal language, or 'jargon' as it is sometimes called, can be extremely difficult for the lay person to understand. This can lead to communication difficulties that have disastrous consequences for those involved. Linguists working in this area are interested in helping people to understand this jargon so that they do not 'trip up' linguistically and end up in prison. In a related field of study, which is sometimes referred to as forensic linguistics, researchers use linguistic tools to identify, for example, the likely authorship of blackmail notes, suicide notes and disputed plagiarism cases. Their evidence is sometimes used in court to establish whether or not it is likely that a person accused of writing for instance a blackmail letter did in fact write the letter, on the basis of linguistic comparisons made with other pieces of writing that they have produced (Eagleson 1994). These comparisons are based not just on the handwriting itself (if indeed the letter has been handwritten) but also on the writer's typical choices of vocabulary, collocation and phraseological patterning. It is worth noting at this point that authorship attribution is also well established in historical literary studies.

A well-known case of forensic linguistic intervention, cited by Olsson (2009), involves an investigation into the disappearance of a teenage girl from her home in Yorkshire. Since her disappearance her parents had been receiving texts from her mobile phone, but the police suspected that they may have been sent by her abductor in order to create the impression that she had left home voluntarily. A forensic linguist who was involved with the case observed that these texts were substantially longer than those that had been sent by the girl before she disappeared, and there were also significant differences in style. For example, whereas the girl tended to leave few spaces in her texts, using phrases like 'ave2go' to mean 'have to go', the texts that her parents had been receiving contained gaps between words, as in: 'ave 2 go'. The texts also contained abbreviations such as 'didn't' and 'aint' which the girl herself tended not to use. They also featured words such as 'mite' instead of 'might', and 'of' instead of 'off'. The identification of these small linguistic differences eventually led to the arrest of the girl's boyfriend. They were found to be features of his texting style rather than hers; he subsequently confessed to having faked the texts and was eventually jailed for her abduction and murder.

Sometimes forensic linguists have used linguistic data to show that evidence has been fabricated by the police. They have been able to demonstrate this by pointing out cases where the police have used words and expressions that the suspect would never themselves have used. For example, evidence provided by the eminent forensic linguist Malcolm Coulthard (1994) was instrumental in securing the release of the 'Birmingham Six'; a group of innocent men who had been wrongfully imprisoned for planting a terrorist bomb in the centre of the second largest city in the UK. Coulthard was able to establish that the so-called 'confessions' used to secure the convictions of these men had been fabricated by the police by pointing out a number of features of the language in the confessions that are characteristic of written rather than spoken discourse, and that would never have been used by these men.

How applied linguistics has contributed to cross-cultural understanding

With its contrast between the informal spoken grammar of everyday discourse on the one hand, and the bureaucratic written language of police documents on the other, the case study discussed at the end of the last section has much in common with another strand of research in applied linguistics, which focuses on the phenomenon of cross-cultural communication. Findings from this research have shown that people from different cultures have different communication patterns and different world views, and that these can affect how they communicate with one another. Before continuing, it is important to look at how 'culture' is defined in applied linguistics. Although it can be applied to people living in different parts of the world, who happen to speak different languages, it can be applied equally well to people belonging to different discourse communities all of whom speak broadly the same language and who live in the same geographical area. For example, factory workers living in Detroit could be said to constitute a different culture from that of a group of lawyers living on the Upper East Side of Manhattan. Although they will have much in common by virtue of the fact that they all live in the USA and all speak English, they will have much that differentiates them making it difficult for them to understand one another at times as they lack shared points of reference. At an even more local level, a group of teachers working in a particular elementary school in the suburbs of any city could be described as a 'discourse community' with its own school-specific vocabulary, its own points of reference, and its own particular culture. Staff from this particular school may at times have difficulties in making themselves understood by teachers from another school which may have slightly different points of reference. The reason why this becomes an issue for linguists is that actual words that we use when communicating will always underspecify the meaning we wish to convey. In order to be understood we rely on a wealth of shared knowledge which we expect our interlocutor to draw on in order for successful communication to take place. This knowledge will include expectations about the type of things we are going to be talking about, expectations about the typical structures and patterns that we will use as well as content knowledge that will be assumed and which does not therefore have to be explicitly stated.

So what kinds of things have linguists discovered about cross-cultural differences in communication patterns, and how have they attempted to resolve these differences? Researchers working in business communication have found significant differences in negotiating styles as well as in the way they conduct themselves in meetings and negotiations. For example, Grinsted (1997) studied the use of jokes in Spanish and Danish business negotiations. She found that Danes were more likely to make themselves the butt of their own jokes, whereas Spanish negotiators were more likely to make others the butt of their jokes. Neither of these approaches to joke telling is intrinsically 'right' or 'wrong' but knowledge of these types of differences may prevent serious misunderstandings in international business negotiations. Findings such as these have already been incorporated into business training materials and courses (see, for example, Rodgers 1997; Viney and Viney 1996; Koester et al. forthcoming).

Applied linguistics also has a great deal to say about cross-cultural communication between people who speak the same language. A recent and very striking example of this is Cameron's (2008) study of the language used in conversations between the daughter of a British politician who was killed by an Irish Republican Army bomb and one of the bombers who killed her father. Cameron focuses in particular on the participants' use of metaphor in these conversations. She observes that although the participants in the conversations are coming from very different starting points, they are able to use metaphor to find points they have in common, and through this use of metaphor they are able to reach a degree of mutual understanding. For example, they both use journey metaphors and metaphors related to pain and healing to describe their respective experiences and they carefully manipulate these metaphors to negotiate the path towards understanding. They also talk about building bridges, but are careful to emphasise that the bridge has 'two ends' to underline the fact that they have very different starting points. Thus through the careful use of metaphor, they are able to reach a degree of understanding.

Cameron has gone on from this study to develop an applied linguistic research project entitled 'Living with Uncertainties'. This project looks at communication between people who hold very different attitudes and beliefs from each other which may be difficult to both parties to accept. She is interested in looking at how employing metaphor to build empathy opens up possibilities for alternative responses to uncertainty than apathy, hardening of attitudes or violence. Her argument is that empathy is essentially constructed, negotiated and resisted through discourse. Accordingly, her studies focus on the everyday language of social interaction as well as the rhetoric of politicians. The programme of research into the dynamics of empathy thus takes in the role of language, and in particular metaphor, in the construction and shifting of people's attitudes to others. The research has implications for how official communication, media discourse and fiction contribute to fostering empathy and building positive relations between social groups.

Conclusion

In this chapter we have looked at just a few of the ways in which applied linguistic research has had a real impact in different walks of life beyond the realms of academia. As we have seen, this desire to engage with – and be accountable to – the wider public is one of the hallmarks of applied linguistics as a field of study, and is one of the main reasons why applied linguistics is such a dynamic and exciting field to be involved in.

This is not to say that applied linguistics is a purely practical endeavour, however. On the contrary, applied linguistics remains an academic subject first and foremost, and in the next chapter we will take a closer look at what studying applied linguistics at university level actually involves.

Studying
applied linguistics

Introduction

So far, we have concentrated on the question of what kind of subject applied linguistics is, and what topic areas it covers. In this chapter we turn to the equally important question of *how* you will study applied linguistics. What kinds of activities will you find yourself doing as an applied linguistics student, and why are you required to do them? We will also consider the very practical question of what career opportunities a degree in applied linguistics can offer you.

What do applied linguistics students do?

As a student of applied linguistics you will engage in a diverse range of study activities. In this section we will discuss and offer advice on the most important of these activities: reading, listening, thinking, writing and researching.

Reading, listening, and (critical) thinking

Wherever and whenever you begin your course of studies in applied linguistics, you can be very sure of one thing: you will be expected to do *a lot* of reading. In fact, you will probably find that reading is the dominant activity that you will engage in throughout your studies, whether you are studying on campus or by some form of distance education. A lot of this reading will be linked to the particular topics covered by lectures or seminars, but you should not restrict yourself only to those readings that are required or recommended by your class teacher or course materials. On the contrary, in order to get the most out of your studies it is crucial that you read as much, and as widely, as you can.

In one sense, this advice is so obvious that it hardly seems worth mentioning; reading is one of the main ways in which we increase our knowledge about any subject, so it follows that a university programme is going to involve a lot of reading. But there is more to academic reading than simply aiming to increase your stock of knowledge about a particular subject. Rather, the point of knowing a lot about an academic subject is that it helps you to *think critically* about it. 'Critical thinking' is the ability to evaluate particular ideas, arguments and courses of action, and it is critical thinking, rather than just an encyclopaedic knowledge of facts, that is valued in higher education. Indeed, in very large part you will eventually be assessed on the basis of your ability to think critically about issues in applied linguistics, and to express these thoughts in writing. (We will say more about the activity of writing later.)

Students often say (and are sometimes told) that they lack the ability to think critically, but this is not true. Critical thinking is part and parcel of everyday life; it is something that everyone does every day. Consider, for example, the last time you bought a mobile phone. Did you just walk into a shop and buy the first phone that you saw? Probably not. It is much more likely that you spent quite a lot of time looking at different models and thinking about the advantages and disadvantages of each before making your decision. You will probably also have visited more than one shop before parting with your money. It is also very likely that you may have treated the advice of the salesperson in each shop you visited with a certain amount of scepticism, and you may well also have done Internet searches and talked to friends about different companies and service providers before even setting off on your shopping trip in the first place. All of this information will have helped you to make your final decision, and your use of this information is essentially a form of critical thinking.

When students say that they cannot think critically, therefore, what they are really saying is that they do not know enough about a topic to be able to evaluate what any individual author says about it. You may well find yourself unable to critically evaluate the point of view expressed by the first book or article that you read on a new subject in applied linguistics, but this is hardly surprising: you will probably have little or nothing to compare it with. You may then find yourself in the even more worrying position of agreeing with the point of view expressed by a second author, even though you might be able to see that this author's point of view is very different from (and perhaps even contradicts) that of the first author you read. But as you read more books and articles by a wider range of authors, you will begin to see individual texts for what they are: not as statements of fact, but as points of view, which may be challenged or supported by things that other authors have written. You will then find that you no longer agree with everyone, and that you have begun to feel more convinced by certain arguments and positions, and less convinced by others. In short, you will have begun to think critically about a topic in applied linguistics. In relation to critical thinking, then, reading brings knowledge, and knowledge brings critical power, and it is for this reason that you need to read as much and as widely as you can.

Before moving on, we need to consider the different types of reading (and listening) material available to you as an applied linguistics student. Perhaps the most familiar type of academic publication is the textbook. Textbooks are of course very useful as introductions to particular subject areas, and an extremely useful resource for developing critical thinking, in that they help you to see what the main positions are in relation to a particular question, problem or issue. But you should not regard textbooks as the last word on any topic in applied linguistics. On the contrary, textbooks are in some respects the least important type of publication in applied linguistics, particularly at postgraduate level. They tell you how research in a particular area has developed over time, what current approaches exist and what the current consensus (if any) is, but by their very nature they do not present you with the cutting-edge research and arguments that you need to be aware of, and which need to be the focus of your own writing and research work. For these, you need to look at articles in academic journals.

Journals are the most important publications in applied linguistics (and in most other academic subject areas) as they contain new research findings and act as the main public forum in which current debates and controversies are played out. We list some of the most important applied linguistics journals in Appendix 1 at the back of this book. Some are wide ranging with occasional special issues devoted to single topics; others are more specialised. Similar to special issues are edited collections – books on a particular topic, where each chapter looks at a different aspect of the main theme, and is usually written by a different author.

Nowadays most people do not read journals in their physical, printed form, but access them online instead, and read and store them on computers and other electronic devices. Although some students (and academics!) still prefer to print out and keep copies of articles in hard copy form, the ability to store articles in electronic form is a major advance in more than one way. First of all, where once you would have had to store your photocopied articles in a tottering pile (or in an ever-expanding set of box files), you can now store your entire collection of papers on a web server, or on a tiny storage drive that you can carry around in your pocket. Furthermore, storing articles electronically means that it is much easier to organise them, find them and search through them as the need arises. The main problem with journals is keeping up with them; there are many journals that cover topics relevant to applied linguists, and most are published three or four times a year. We therefore recommend that you sign up for content alerts using the utilities provided on the websites of most of the major journals. When you do this, a list of contents is automatically emailed to you every time a new issue of a journal is published, and you can quickly see whether this latest issue contains any articles that sound particularly relevant or interesting to you, and which would therefore be worth reading.

Most of the journals that we mention in Appendix 1 are only accessible via a paid subscription, but there are also some open-access ones available via the Internet too. Some of these are very good, but you need to be wary of any journal that does not have an editorial board that includes recognised authorities in the field, a peer-review process (i.e. a process whereby articles have to be 'vetted' and approved by other academics before they can be accepted for publication) or an ISSN number. Most of all, we would advise you against relying on Wikipedia and other informal and unregulated Internet sources. Wikipedia is certainly a wonderful resource, but it is also notoriously unreliable: it is always changing, and it is often very biased, and sometimes just plain wrong. For example, Wikipedia currently classifies the discipline of computational linguistics as a branch of applied linguistics, when it is actually a branch of computer science that has at least as much in common with applied mathematics as it does with applied linguistics!

So far we have focused on the kinds of reading that you will be doing as an applied linguistics student, but you will no doubt have noticed that we included the word 'listening' in the heading of this section as well. This is because there is now also an ever-expanding range of podcast and vodcast resources available on the Internet, via portals such as YouTube and iTunes. Similar caveats to those expressed above about electronic written sources also apply here. That is, you should feel free to use these resources, but you should at the same time treat them as points of view rather than statements of fact, and you probably should not cite them or quote from them in your own papers, unless the podcaster is a world-famous leading authority – and even then it's better to quote from books and articles that they have written, as these are considered more definitive and reliable.

Discussing

Essentially the same points that we made about why you need to read a lot also apply to lectures: it is a good idea to attend as many as possible, listen attentively, and think critically about what you have heard. Ask yourself how the content of a lecture relates to the content of previous lectures that you have attended, and how it relates to the books and articles that you may already have read on the subject. However, it is also important to be aware that the taught component of many applied linguistics courses is based primarily on seminars rather than lectures. The point of seminars is to give you an opportunity to interact with your teacher and your peers, and to discuss and ask questions, not just listen in silence. This is also part and parcel of learning the skill of critical thinking; seminar discussions give you the opportunity to test ideas out, by examining them in detail and attempting to identify their weaknesses and strengths. Talking about ideas also helps to consolidate them in your mind; in this sense, seminar discussions are rather like play rehearsals. Just as rehearsals give the actors in a play a chance to learn their lines, seminars give you a chance to develop a fluent command of the concepts and terminology used in a particular topic in applied linguistics.

You may feel uncomfortable about participating in seminar discussions at first, but it is much better to join in while the seminar is in progress than it is to approach the teacher at the end of class with a list of questions about the content of the session. The whole purpose of the seminar as a mode of academic interaction is to give you the opportunity to ask questions, so it is entirely expected that you should do this during the seminar, and not after it has finished. Also, if you ask questions during the seminar, the whole class can benefit from them.

Whether you are studying on campus or as a distance student you should also participate in online forums and discussion groups that relate to your own areas of study. Many lists are public ones but some (e.g. the Corpora list for corpus linguistics) can be highly specialised, and do not always welcome contributors who post very basic questions, Nevertheless, once you have got beyond the basics these specialised lists can be very rich and rewarding resources, especially if you are planning to study a particular topic in more depth. It is now also increasingly common for university applied linguistics programmes to have their own discussion lists, accessed via Virtual Learning Environments (VLEs). We strongly recommend you make extensive use of these. Some students also set up their own groups using Internet resources such as Google, Yahoo and Skype.

Writing

Students often think of writing only as a form of assessment. However, while it is certainly true that most applied linguistics assessments are in the form of written assignments, university teachers do not set these merely as a test or ordeal – even though there may be times when you might suspect this to be the case! The most important reason for setting written assignment tasks is that they are where the real learning takes place, or at least where your prior learning is consolidated. Writing an assignment gives you the opportunity to set out and justify your own position on a particular topic in applied linguistics. Doing this challenges you to be extremely clear and explicit – it confronts you with the fact that your ideas are not always as clear or as strong as you thought they were, and thus forces you to think again about your own beliefs. This is why most applied linguistics courses prefer to set written assignments rather than 'short-answer' forms of assessment such as multiple-choice exams. These are good for testing students' knowledge of facts, but they are not so good at helping students to develop the skill of constructing cogent arguments in relation to problems, questions and issues in applied linguistics.

There are now very many books on the market that offer detailed discussions of how to write academic essays in the humanities and social sciences (where applied linguistics sits), and in Appendix 2 at the end of this book we list some resources that we think are particularly useful and relevant to applied linguistics students. Here, we will simply offer four very general (but we believe still very important and useful) pieces of advice about writing assignments. First of all, check at regular intervals whether you are answering the question that has been set for you, or which you have set for yourself. This may seem like very obvious advice indeed, but in our experience this is still one of the most common traps that students fall into. The best way to check that you are answering the question is to look back at the question very regularly while you are writing your assignment, and ask yourself how the section of the assignment that you happen to be working on at the time contributes to providing an answer to it. You should also check that your introduction and conclusion match each other before you submit your work: ideally, your conclusion should bring you back to the place from which you started off in your introduction, and should provide answers to the questions that you set yourself at the beginning. If your conclusion seems to be talking about something different, then there is a problem!

Second, and on a related note, it is important to avoid padding out your essay with irrelevant or over-general material. Again, this piece of advice may seem self-evident on the face of it, but in fact there is quite a high degree of skill involved in getting the balance right in deciding how general or specific you should be in terms of the information you provide in academic assignments, whether at undergraduate or postgraduate level. On the one hand, the assignment genre asks you to imagine that you are writing for an intelligent but non-expert reader, which suggests that you need to provide quite a lot of background information. But on the other hand, if you provide too much background information you may find your work being criticised for spending too much time on background issues and not getting on with the main job of answering the question. We cannot provide you with any convenient 'rule-of-thumb' for deciding where the balance lies in this regard; all we can do is flag it up as an issue that you need to be aware of, and as a skill that you will almost certainly develop naturally as you progress through your studies. The more practised you become as an academic writer and the more knowledgeable you become in your chosen field of studies, the more you will develop an instinctive 'feel' for what is and is not relevant to a particular assignment question.

Our third piece of advice is that you should make sure that your own voice and ideas always occupy 'centre-stage' in your writing. While it is of course important to demonstrate in your essay that you have read and understood what previous researchers and leading authorities have said on a particular topic, your main task is to establish and justify your own position on a particular question, problem or issue in applied linguistics. There is no need for you to do this by fronting your own arguments with 'I think' or 'in my opinion' – your reader will assume that everything in your essay is your opinion unless you tell them otherwise, by explicitly attributing a particular statement to another author. Similarly, whenever you report what someone else says, you need to go on at some subsequent point to tell your reader whether you agree with this statement or not, or at least why you have mentioned it in the first place, and how it relates to the argument that you are making. If you do not do this, your assignment will seem like a patchwork of other author's voices, and you may be criticised for producing work that is too descriptive, and not 'critical' or 'analytical' enough. One way of making your voice more prominent in your essay is to put the ideas first and the source of the ideas in brackets afterwards. In other words, the sentence:

> The majority of the communicative interactions that take place in English around the world are between non-native speakers, and not between native and non-native speakers of the language (Seidlhofer 2005).

sounds much more authoritative than the sentence:

> Seidlhofer (2005) reports that the majority of the communicative interactions that take place in English around the world are between non-native speakers, and not between native and non-native speakers of the language.

The key difference between these two sentences is that the first one highlights the information, whereas the second highlights the original author. In other words, the first sentence tells the reader something about communicative interactions that take place in English around the world, and includes a citation that tells the reader where this information comes from. The main point of the second sentence, in contrast, is to tell the reader that Seidlhofer has reported something on this topic. It does not tell the reader whether the writer agrees or disagrees with what Seidlhofer says, or even why the writer is reporting Seidlhofer's statement at this point; the writer must go on to establish these points subsequently. Of course, there is no reason why you cannot do this in most cases, and we are certainly not advising you not to use this 'author-first' citation style in your own writing. On the contrary, it is an integral feature of academic writing, and is an essential textual resource if you want to discuss the work of an individual writer in any depth. What we do suggest, however, is that you should avoid using this 'author-first' citation style too much in your writing, as this may give your readers (and assessors!) the impression that you are just summarising the views of other authors, and failing to state your own position on the particular topic, question or issue that you are discussing (Groom 2000; Ridley 2008).

Another way of sounding authoritative is to vary the reporting verbs that you use when referring to other's people's work. If you agree strongly with a particular finding or viewpoint, and want to emphasise its importance, you can indicate this by choosing an appropriate reporting verb, such as 'show' or 'demonstrate', instead of a more neutral reporting verb such as 'state' or 'say'. If, on the other hand, you are more cautious about the finding or viewpoint, you should use more tentative reporting verbs, such as 'claim' or 'contend'. Remember, however, that if you do this, you will still have to indicate your own position in relation to the cited statement at some subsequent point in your text. We would also advise you not to use the reporting verb 'prove' unless you are putting the word 'not' in front of it, as things are never proven beyond doubt in applied linguistics! Finally, and leading on from all of this, it is essential that you explicitly acknowledge all of your secondary sources by citing them in one of the ways indicated above. If you do not do this you may find yourself being accused of plagiarism.

When writing assignments in applied linguistics, it is important to write analytically rather than simply descriptively. Writing analytically involves putting forward your own ideas, seeing relationships and contradictions between the ideas of others, breaking ideas down into their constituent parts and seeing how theories can be applied to real situations. It also involves the ability to see the strengths and weaknesses in your own and other authors' ideas and, perhaps most importantly, managing to convince the reader of the validity of your own viewpoint. This involves making a series of claims, each supported by pieces of evidence. Claims include 'claims of fact' (e.g. 'metaphor is pervasive in written and spoken language), 'claims of value' (e.g. 'essays that contain metaphor are more stylish than ones that do not') and claims of policy (e.g. 'language learners should be taught to use metaphor in the foreign language'). 'Claims of fact' can generally be proven or disproven, whereas 'claims of value' and 'claims of policy' cannot. It is best to put the claims at the beginning of one's sentences and paragraphs as they stand out better this way. Claims must then be supported with evidence. Types of evidence can include research studies, statistics, logical explanations, analogies, facts, references to authorities and personal experience. The last two types of evidence are generally considered the weakest and often need to be complemented by other types of evidence. Citing authorities simply amounts to saying 'X is true because this famous applied linguist says so'. This kind of argument is not generally considered sufficient at postgraduate level. Equally, if your evidence consists entirely of what you yourself may have witnessed in your own personal experience, no one can verify whether or not it is actually true. In both cases, it would be best to provide an additional source of evidence in support of your particular claim.

Student assignments in applied linguistics tend to proceed from claim to claim, building up a particular 'story', and in many cases begin with a justification for the particular piece of research or line of reasoning that the rest of the assignment will report on or develop. For example, the claims about metaphor listed in the previous paragraph might be incorporated into the literature review of an essay where it is claimed (a) that metaphor is ubiquitous; (b) that the ability to use metaphor makes language learners sound better; (c) that learners often do not know how to use metaphor in the target language; and (d) that learners should therefore be taught how to do so. The essay might then go on to propose a way in which learners might be taught to use metaphor, contrast this with previous approaches and say why this particular approach may be better. It could then describe a small-scale study where the student has tested out their hypothesis. In fact, what we have just described here is an essay that was produced by one of the students on our MA programme. This particular student then went on to explore her metaphor-testing technique in more depth in her dissertation research project. In this project she tested out the teaching technique on a larger number of students and conducted statistical analyses to ascertain whether or not it was effective.

Researching

In very general terms, research in applied linguistics takes two forms. One is based on the analysis and critique of other people's work and ideas; the other involves doing an original research project of your own. Most applied linguistics programmes require you to carry out at least one independent research project during the course of your studies. Usually this is written up in the *dissertation* (as it is called in some varieties of English) or *thesis* (as it is called in some other varieties of English) that forms the culmination of your studies, although some students do research work for coursework assignments too. Here you really are 'doing' applied linguistics, in that you will be required to identify a problem that you think needs to be addressed, and you will attempt to solve or at least offer a contribution towards improving understandings of it. The process starts with your own reading; as you read about research carried out by other people in the field, you will find out not only what has been said and done already, but also what still remains in doubt or open to question, and your own work will attempt to fill this 'knowledge gap' that you have identified. This is yet another aspect of 'critical thinking' – the ability to spot a gap in the research literature, or to perceive a problem where everyone else thinks no problem exists; that is, to 'problematise' or disturb the consensus in some innovative and constructive way.

An interesting feature (and we think one of the strengths) of applied linguistics is that most if not all of the questions, problems and issues that it focuses on can be investigated in more than one way. In fact, it is possible to put this in much stronger terms, by saying that most if not all of the questions, problems and issues that applied linguistics focuses on cannot fully be understood *unless* they are investigated from a variety of different theoretical and methodological perspectives. This is reflected in the very diverse range of research methodologies that applied linguists use. We will look at these different research methodologies in detail in Chapters 5 to 10 of this book.

What can I do with an applied linguistics qualification?

Absolutely the best reason for embarking on a course of studies in any subject at university is simply that you are interested in it. If you are interested in a subject you will enjoy studying it, and this enjoyment will be its own reward. But people very often do degrees for other reasons too – notably, in order to get into a profession, or to progress within the profession where they are already working – so it is entirely reasonable for students and potential students of applied linguistics to ask what a course of study in the subject can do for them in material terms.

In answering this question it is useful to begin by stating clearly what a degree in applied linguistics *cannot* do for you. Although textbooks and reference sources often include subjects such as translation, clinical linguistics, speech therapy, deaf linguistics and lexicography under the general rubric of applied linguistics, a degree in applied linguistics will not qualify you to work as a speech therapist, lexicographer or translator. If you want to pursue one of these careers then you need to take a vocational course of studies in one of these highly specialized areas instead.

However, while it is certainly true that applied linguistics is not a vocational subject like speech therapy or translation (or like dentistry or law, for that matter) the 'real-world' orientation of applied linguistics means that is not a non-vocational, 'pure' academic subject like history, sociology or astrophysics either. This is particularly true with regard to the long and still vibrant and centrally important relationship that applied linguistics has with the English language teaching profession. Probably the largest single group of people enrolled on any applied linguistics programme will be EFL teachers who are studying for a higher degree in order to secure better paid and more fulfilling jobs. Although a degree in applied linguistics is not officially recognised as a teaching qualification per se in most countries, it does constitute one of the most popular and prestigious avenues for professional development among practising language teachers, and particularly among those who want to work in universities.

While EFL teachers still form a large part of every MA applied linguistics cohort at our own institution, for example, we find that they are now being joined by increasing numbers of students who come from, or are aiming to enter into, other academic and professional backgrounds. Prominent among these are mainstream school teachers and people who have worked or who aspire to work in media industries such as radio and TV broadcasting, print journalism, book publishing, advertising or marketing. We are also seeing increasing numbers of students who have come straight from undergraduate degrees in subjects as diverse as literature, linguistics, politics, psychology, sociology, anthropology and cultural studies. This also helps to explain why applied linguistics degrees themselves have also begun to diversify in recent years. Originally, programmes in applied linguistics were only offered at postgraduate level because they were exclusively aimed at experienced teachers wanting to upgrade their professional qualifications. As the scope of applied linguistics has dramatically expanded in recent years (as discussed in Chapter 1), an increasing number of universities are starting to offer BA degrees in applied linguistics, as there is now less need for students to have prior experience as teachers in order to make sense of the subject.

Conclusion

The aim of this chapter has been to furnish you with some practical advice about the principal activities that are involved in studying applied linguistics at university, and about what studying applied linguistics can (and cannot) do for you in career terms. From here onwards, our discussion will focus in more detail on what is involved in carrying out applied linguistics research projects of various kinds. Our aim will be to help you to understand the principles that underpin each of these various research methods and approaches. In so doing, we hope that you will be able to critically evaluate the published research papers that you will spend so much time reading in the course of your studies, and that you will also be able to carry out and write-up well-designed and carefully-implemented research projects of your own.

5

Collecting qualitative data

Introduction

The focus of this chapter and the next is on qualitative data collected via interviews, case studies, classroom observation schedules and other observational procedures. The chapter begins by considering the nature of qualitative data and what it tells us about the aims of qualitative research. We then look in more detail at some examples of the most important and widely used qualitative data collection procedures and protocols. Some of these are published research studies, whereas others are accounts of postgraduate research conducted at MA and PhD level. Full reports of some of these unpublished studies are available on the e-resources website for this book. The chapter concludes with a discussion of some of the key ethical issues that often arise in qualitative research.

The nature of qualitative data

The popular perception of academic work is that it always involves the collection and analysis of quantitative data: numbers, percentages, statistics, graphs and charts. While it is certainly true that some research in applied linguistics does indeed focus on such data (as we will see later in this book), there is another tradition of research in applied linguistics that does not concern itself with quantitative data at all. To the non-expert observer, this other 'research paradigm' can seem to consist of little more than detailed descriptions of things that people do and say, with some interpretation added on to the end. However, this approach is much more complex and rigorous than may at first seem. This qualitative paradigm calls for a completely different way of thinking about what counts as academic knowledge, and a different set of questions.

The main difference between qualitative and quantitative approaches to research is that, whereas quantitative approaches involve numbers, qualitative approaches do not. Whereas in quantitative research, the aim is often to make generalisations about large populations, qualitative research is more usually interested in providing detailed descriptions of smaller groups of individuals. Qualitative research tends to answer questions about *how* and *why*, rather than *what*. Whereas quantitative research is often interested in simplicity and elegance, qualitative research is interested in the more authentic messier side of the human experience; rather than 'papering over cracks' it will try to offer a detailed examination of the cracks. Whereas in quantitative research the aim is often to control or eliminate as many variables as possible, in order to focus on just one or two 'key' variables, in qualitative research a wider range of variables is usually of (at least) potential interest. Whereas the aim of many quantitative studies is to identify a sample of 'typical' participants and to generalise from this sample to a larger population, the aim in qualitative research is to find individuals who can provide rich and varied data that shed new or interesting light on the phenomenon under investigation. In many ways qualitative data are a more accurate way of describing the non-linear relationships that exist within the complex systems that humans create. In qualitative research, phenomena are presented as interconnected rather than causally related discrete entities. Therefore qualitative researchers will often begin with a loose research question or a problem that needs to be addressed, and refine it as they go along. Accordingly, the distinction between data collection and analysis is not as clear-cut as it is within the quantitative paradigm. Quantitative researchers tend to set themselves an objective research question, gather the data needed, and analyse these data in order to answer the question. Qualitative researchers, on the other hand, are not always looking for objective answers to specific questions. Rather the process is more iterative with research questions being continually refined as the data are examined, and then the data examined in the light of the refined research question. To sum up, whereas the quantitative researcher might be interested in wide but fairly shallow coverage of the data, the qualitative researcher is interested in detailed, thick descriptions of smaller data sets. Whereas in quantitative research, objectivity is paramount, in qualitative research, subjectivity is foregrounded. Data are sometimes deliberately chosen to present a subjective view of the phenomenon being studied. The subjectivity can be that of the researcher or of the participants in the study.

Qualitative data are sometimes used to complement quantitative findings by means of illustration and deepening the analysis, incorporating complexity and thus providing a more realistic way of seeing things, but as we will see below, this not the only way of combining the two approaches. Indeed, qualitative research often stands alone without being complemented by quantitative data at all.

Interviews

One of the most popular ways of finding out what people think and feel about something is simply to ask them direct questions about it. In applied linguistics and the social sciences more generally, this kind of data collection strategy is normally referred to as interview research. Three main kinds of interview tend be used in applied linguistic research: structured, unstructured and semi-structured. In structured interviews, the interviewer organizes the content and procedures in advance and then has little freedom to make modifications. Unstructured interviews have more flexibility and freedom. Semi-structured interviews have some of the characteristics of both and are thus a sort of halfway house.

Whichever form of interview is used, it is important for the interviewer to engage in active listening throughout the course of an interview. This involves showing the interviewee that you are interested in and engaging with what they have to say. Active listening techniques can include: repeating occasional phrases used by the interviewee for clarification, paraphrasing, clarifying, summarising and, when necessary, remaining silent. The questions asked should not be leading or too biased.

A novel approach to interviewing in language teaching research was employed by Tatsumoto (2010) in her PhD research. She was interested in assessing the relationships that students perceived between peer cooperation, motivation, self-confidence and their level of English, before and after an English language training programme that had a heavy focus on cooperative learning. She wanted to intervene as little as possible in her students' thought processes, so she simply presented them with the diagram shown at Figure 5.1, and asked them to tell her if they saw any relationships between the phenomena in the four boxes. After they had produced their spontaneous responses she probed further, asking them if they could see any other relationships. The data produced were then transcribed and categorised into different types of responses according to where the interviewees perceived the relationships to be. This semi-structured interview format was particularly suitable for this study as the students needed some prompting but they also needed a degree of freedom to produce data that would be rich and meaningful, as well as free from the researcher's own biases.

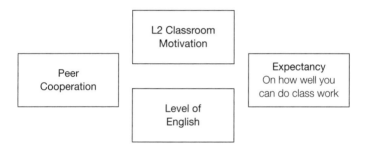

Figure 5.1: **Diagram for interviews at the beginning and the end of cooperative learning in Tatsumoto (2010).**

   The transcription of interview data that has been recorded can be a difficult area for researchers. Sometimes such large quantities of data are produced that the transcribing task is daunting. The best approach in such cases is to listen to the entire recording and to select those aspects that most strongly relate to the research question. There may be areas of the data that do not need to be transcribed.

Introspection: think-aloud, retrospective recall and diary studies

Some qualitative research studies involve asking participants to reflect on their own views, learning processes, or experiences either during or after a particular activity has taken place. When the reflection takes place simultaneously with the activity it is called 'think-aloud'. When it takes place after the event it is referred to as 'retrospective recall'. A particularly good use of the think-aloud technique, producing pertinent and memorable data is made by Slobin (2003) in his study of the different ways in which the language one speaks interacts with one's thought processes. Slobin asked 14 Spanish speakers and 21 American English speakers to give an oral report of the English translation of a passage from Isabel Allende's novel *The House of the Spirits*, as they were reading it. When they provided an oral report of this passage, The American English speakers added a large number of manner-encoded verbs such as 'stumble', 'stagger' and 'trudge' to their reports, such as those shown in Box 5.1.

Box 5.1 **Responses produced by American English speakers in Slobin's (2003) study.**

> *He dodged occasional hazards in the trail; rock from side to side; slosh through; stagger; struggle; stumble, sluggish movement, stumbling over the rocks on the path; slowly edge his way down the trail; slow his pace; take each step slow and difficult, tiring and never-ending; trek; trench through a muddy path; trudge; slowly hobbling.*

Moreover, 95 per cent of these respondents claimed to have mental images of various types of movement. They thus appeared to be focusing heavily on the manner of movement. In contrast, the Spanish speakers reports did not focus on the manner of the movement and only 14 per cent reported having images of movement, although they did visualise the path, the physical details of the surroundings, the man's inner state, and his trajectory of movement. Typical comments from the Spanish-speaking informants' think-aloud transcripts are shown in Box 5.2.

Box 5.2 **Responses produced by Spanish speakers in Slobin's (2003) study.**

I see him walking with difficulty, with care not to slip, making especially slow movements, as if it cost him special effort to move his legs or was carrying a weight in them. It was hard for him to walk through the mud hole. 'I don't picture him getting down from the train but rather standing still on the platform and I don't see him going along a very long trajectory in order to arrive at the village; rather I see him at a distance from it, looking at it. I repeat that I don't observe him moving in the direction of the village but rather as static images, more like photographs.' (Chilean)

It would seem that he moves, walks, but I don't see any sort of detailed action on his part. I know that he walks and must have his feet burdened with the stony ground but I see the stones and the path more than the manner in which he walks. … It would seem that he were floating at times as if he were seated in a cart.' (Mexican)

Interestingly, there were a few bilingual subjects in the experiment who reported distinctly different imagery in their two languages, with more manner of movement imagery when reporting on the text in English than in Spanish, but still much less than the monolingual speakers of English, as we can see in Box 5.3.

Box 5.3 **A response produced by a bilingual participant in Slobin's (2003) study.**

> *I'm still seeing very little manner of movement but I see more concrete walking and I can sort of make out a pace. I see less of the surroundings. The story feels different. There is less detail in regards to the scenery. (Mexican bilingual).*

Slobin used his findings to suggest that the way in which one language encodes manner of movement has a significant effect on those aspects of the context that people perceive as being pertinent, and that they have difficulty envisaging those aspects of the context that are downplayed by their native language. We can see here that he has selected the most pertinent comments made by his informants to illustrate his point. He will also have analysed the data to ensure that the responses of the English speakers were indeed more likely to be characterised by manner of movement verbs than those of the Spanish speakers. This will have been done by means of data categorisation, a process that we will discuss in detail in Chapter 6. One of the problems with think-aloud techniques is that participants may not always be sure about their own thought processes and thought processes themselves can be very difficult to articulate. However, if the researcher is aware of these limitations, the techniques can be very productive.

A second research technique that provokes introspection is retrospective recall. Here the participant is asked to think about the thought processes that they had been employing during a particular activity. Again, there are issues of reliability and to some extent they are exacerbated by the fact that time has passed since the activity. On the other hand, retrospective recall does have an advantage in that it does not interfere with the activity itself at the time. It can therefore play a crucial role in a research study. An example of the sort of research question that can be investigated through retrospective recall is shown in Box 5.4, where we reproduce a genuine question from a teacher/researcher.

Box 5.4 **Question posed by a language teacher/researcher.**

I had an interesting experience the other day that's made me think there might be a very important factor worth investigating in terms of language transfer that I hadn't considered before. I have a class of teenagers who are doing Cambridge FCE this year, so they're about B2 level, and they also study German. Only one of them came to the lesson, though, so I thought we'd just do some speaking practice. So I started by saying 'Tell me about your life', and she said 'I think my life is quite normal. My parents sind ...' ('sind' being the 3rd person plural of 'be' in German). She laughed and I asked her why she would have got something so fundamental as 'be' confused, and she explained that what she wanted to say was that her parents are divorced, only she didn't know the word 'divorced' in English, but she thought she did in German - not that she was actually going to say the German word, but just that that was the direction her mind had taken. (In the end when I asked her she couldn't actually remember it in German either.)

So what seemed to have happened is that she was searching for a word in English to match the concept 'divorced', couldn't find it but for some reason then went to German (makes me think that maybe she activated a non-L1 node, rather than separate non-Italian and non-German nodes?), but that was actually happening while she was processing the verb 'be', so that got processed wrongly. Very interesting in my opinion! Do you know if there is a term for this kind of forward planning we do when we produce language? I think the problem might have been exacerbated by the fact that she couldn't remember the German word either, as perhaps the extra processing required to try and think of it made the language switch effect even stronger.

> *The problem for me is that to investigate this kind of thing would probably mean interrupting the speaker immediately to ask them why they thought they might have got confused. But if it really is a significant factor for cross-language lexical transfer then it might actually distort my results if I don't take it into account.*

In this situation a retrospective recall approach was used in a very informal way when the researcher asked the student why she thought she got confused. However, this example does also highlight one of the problems with retrospective recall. We have no way of knowing whether the student will be able to accurately recall what was going through her mind during this class, nor that she will report it completely objectively. Here we may get cases of positive response bias in that she may try to predict what the researcher wants to hear, and simply say that. Retrospective recall data is, by definition, highly subjective.

Both think-aloud and retrospective recall data need to be recorded and transcribed. Again, as with interview data, the key lies in transcribing those parts of the data that are most relevant to the research questions. Not everything will need to be transcribed. If the focus is on the ideas produced, then a loose transcription system can be used. If the focus is on the language used by the speaker then a widely accepted set of transcription conventions needs to be used. These will vary depending on what aspects of the language the researcher is interested in, and are discussed in more detail in Chapter 9, where we look at text analysis.

Another way to obtain introspective data is to ask the participants in the study to keep a diary of how they felt during the study. This approach is particularly useful in language teaching research projects where, for example, the researcher wants to find out what the students really think of a new approach that is being trialled. This technique was employed by Ormeno (2009) in her study of language teacher trainees attending pre-service training courses in Chile. The aim of Ormeno's study was to investigate the benefits of introducing a metacognitive awareness-raising component into the training programme. Metacognitive awareness' is the ability to reflect consciously on what learning strategy you are using to tackle a particular learning problem, and to evaluate whether this is the best strategy to be using in that context. Ormeno's approach to this question was to compare the progress of a group of trainees that had had this training with a group of trainees that had had more conventional training. As part of her study, Ormeno asked the trainees in the research groups to keep a diary, recording their feelings about the training programme. She was able to use some of these diary entries to add qualitative support to her quantitative finding that the metacognitive awareness training was indeed beneficial, but some of the diary entries revealed unexpected results, as we can see in Box 5.5.

Box 5.5 Extract from one of the diary entries in Ormeno's (2009) study.

> 'Everything was OK until teacher was hostile when she referred to me as "these kind of people" at the moment she was given an example about rude guys, and she even emphasised her opinion telling to my classmates something about those guys who were saying swear words ... I think it was not my day because I felt completely ashamed.'
>
> Diary entry November 2006, day not recorded.)

Ormeno herself was the teacher of this class and had no recollection of the incident, except that she may have waved her hand generally in the direction of that student while she had been talking. This example shows how diary entries can reveal qualitative data that may impact heavily on the quantitative outcomes of the study, and which the researcher could never have known about otherwise.

Case studies

Case studies are in-depth analyses of individual cases designed to provide answers to a certain research question. A good example of applied linguistic research using a case study approach is Myers' (1995) investigation of how scientists, who are used to writing academic articles, have to learn to adapt their writing style when they need to start applying for patents for their inventions. In order to do this, Myers shadowed two scientists, a zoologist and a neurosurgeon, and looked at a number of drafts and redrafts of their patent applications as they rewrote their proposals in response to reviewers' comments. His main focus was on how people gradually learn to rewrite their ideas for a completely different audience. During his study Myers obtained a great deal of background information about the two scientists, including their educational history, their previous careers, the nature of the inventions that they were attempting to patent, their family history (one of the participants had come from a family of inventors, the other had not), what motivated them, how they believed their inventions would benefit humankind, the conventional patenting procedures within their own institutions and so on. As well as reading through the manuscripts he held regular interviews with the participants and got to know them well. Much of this contextual information proved crucial in helping Myers analyse the language in their proposals.

A good example of a piece of case study research in the language teaching context can be found in Ehrman (1996). Ehrman was interested in finding out what it is that makes language learning more difficult for some students than it is for others. One of her approaches was to use a variety of questionnaires and interviews with students and to put all this data together to build a detailed picture of that student. Figure 5.2 contains an example of Ehrman's 'thick description' of one student, Elsa (not her real name), who was experiencing difficulties in her French classes.

By analysing the data in this thick description, Ehrman was able to conclude that the core of Elsa's problem was not cognitive dysfunction, and that seeing her problem as a 'disability' was misleading. In reality, Elsa had an 'intense affective reaction, almost phobic, towards French' (ibid.: 230), which had caused a downward spiral in response to negative experiences. She also had a strong need to learn the language in meaningful contexts, which was not the case in her current learning situation. It is difficult to see how this sort of complexity could have been investigated using only quantitative approaches.

A key question when selecting participants for case study research is whether you should focus on the 'typical' person or whether you should choose extreme cases. Although Myers does not claim that the scientists he studied are to be regarded as typical, it is nevertheless implicit in his argument that the difficulties he describes are likely to be encountered by other scientists writing patent applications. On the other hand, the participants in Ehrman's study were chosen because they were struggling with the language to an unusual degree, and the aim of the study was to find out why this was so. What both studies do, however, is emphasise the complexity of their given areas of study, and underline the need for the qualitative researcher to consider all possible angles.

Biodata
23 years old
Native speaker of English, American born
Recent BA from good university in international relations
Two languages on entry to graduate level
Diagnosed as dyslexic and 'language learning disabled' while in university

Modern Language Aptitude Test Results
Part 1 (Number learning) 93%
Part 2 (Phonetic script) 83%
Part 3 (Spelling clues) 40%
Part 4 (Words in sentences) 56%
Part 5 (Paired associates) 29%
Total 63% (Average for the program she is in)

Myers Briggs Personality Type Indicator
Preference (consistency) scores very low, and Elsa strongly resisted committing to any category. Strongest preference (though weak) was for intuition.

Hartmann Ego Boundary Questionnaire (orientation towards others)
Thin boundaries 1.5. SD above the mean for females in this language program and nearly 1 SD above Hartman's mean for females. Both internal and external boundaries are thin, meaning that she was sensitive to the needs and opinions of others.

Motivation and Strategies Questionnaire
Rated herself as below average in language ability but expected to perform averagely in class.
Rated herself as not at all motivated in French but very motivated in Polish.
Somewhat more interested in non-Western languages than Western ones.
Really nervous about French, a 'fair amount' of anxiety about learning Polish.

Interview data
Strongly endorsed open-ended language learning activities (e.g. discussions), a small group of conversations, interviews with native speakers, field trips using the target language, correction of written and oral errors, offsite immersion experiences, being forced to use what one knows even if imprecise, using the language as much as possible both in and out of school, and trusting her intuitions.

Strongly rejected learning dialogues by heart, reading aloud one by one after the teacher, hearing grammatical rules explained in the target language, correcting grammar mistakes in the writings, discovering grammar patterns for herself, pronunciation and drill, studying alone, activities that use the hands, background music, taking a lot of notes, and completing one task before beginning another.

A section of the report on Elsa's psychological tests that diagnosed her as learning disabled states that 'one can see … how learning a foreign language would be extremely problematic, even considering her superior intelligence'. For many individuals with this type of language-based disability, learning a foreign language at a professional level is probably out of reach.

Case notes
Elsa was given some trial training in Spanish and she undertook the experiment enthusiastically; the first hour was spent interviewing Elsa about how she learns, and then the Spanish teacher gave her a lesson in Spanish. The main thing she did was to make sure that everything she taught Elsa was in some kind of communicative context. She reported that Elsa learned splendidly, and Elsa was equally positive.

Figure 5.2 A 'thick' description of 'Elsa' (source: Ehrman 1996: 228–231).
Reproduced with permission from Sage Publications.

Observation

Much qualitative research takes place through observation. At its simplest, observation can be defined as simply watching and recording how participants behave and interact in certain situations. However, observation as a research method in applied linguistics is not quite as simple as that. Observers may or may not be part of the action. Therefore we need to make a crucial distinction between participant observation, where the observer is part of the action, and non-participant observation, where the researcher is not part of the action.

Non-participant observation

As the name suggests, non-participant observation requires the researcher to quietly observe what is going on in a particular situation, without being involved in the situation herself or himself. This type of data collection strategy is particularly useful for projects that aim to find out how language teaching classrooms work. It can produce data that are both qualitative and quantitative. For example, by using tick-box classroom observation schedules, the research can obtain quantitative data that can then be analysed statistically.

An alternative approach is to collect descriptive data that can then be analysed qualitatively at a later stage. This approach was taken by Matsumoto (2009) in a study of interaction patterns in Japanese university EFL classrooms. The main aim of Matsumoto's study was to investigate discrepancies between teachers' and students' views of classroom interaction and how these might be reconciled. She used a variety of qualitative research techniques besides classroom observation, some of which will be discussed later in this chapter, but classroom observation constituted the core of her study.

An extract from one of Matsumoto's classroom observations can be seen in Figure 5.3. The aim here was to look at what the teacher was doing, how individual students were behaving, and how groups were being formed at certain points during the session. Matsumoto was able to use these data to pinpoint potential points of conflict in terms of what the teacher was doing and what the students were doing. She then used these potential points of conflict as a basis for interviews with the teacher and the students.

Non-participant observation is also used in research into the effectiveness of language teacher training programmes. One example of this is Ormeno's aforementioned study of teacher trainers in Chile. One of the aims of her study was to assess the extent to which participants in the study were able to incorporate elements of metacognitive awareness training into their own teaching. She therefore made video recordings of their teaching practice sessions and asked three experienced teachers to watch the videos and give a running commentary on what they saw as the strengths and weaknesses of the teacher trainee sessions. The observers had not been informed of the overall aims of the study. Ormeno recorded the commentaries and identified anything said that might indicate that the participants were incorporating the metacognitive awareness training into their own teaching. Some of the more relevant comments are shown in Figure 5.4. Although Ormeno was not able to say that these teaching behaviours were *definitely* a direct result of the training programme, she was able to present them as *possible* examples of the benefits of the training programme.

These behaviours were later classified into six categories:

1   motivational features: engaging students' opinions and making connections to students' lives
2   affective features: showing interest, praising the students' efforts, valuing the students' opinions
3   coaching features (cognitive awareness): prompting and modelling the use of learning strategies, e.g. deduction by using imagery
4   language awareness (cognitive awareness): developing/fostering awareness of how the English language system works
5   autonomy features: allowing freedom for students to decide groupings, allowing students time by themselves but being available for support and feedback,
6   assessment features (metacognitive awareness): encouraging self-assessment, strategy assessment and assessment of materials.

(Ormeno 2009: 299)

In neither of the two studies reviewed above was the observer involved in the actual activity. Matsumoto sat to one side of the classroom and did not participate in the class, and Ormeno had her observers watch videos of the teaching sessions after the event. They are therefore both examples of non-participant observation. In some studies, the observer is actually

Time	Teacher	Individual Students	Groups of students
00:00:00	Coming into the classroom and reminding them about the quiz to be given next week. Taking attendance, calling students' first names.		
00:02:01	Introducing the researcher with the video camera	Each student answers by saying "Yes" in Japanese or English, raising one hand. The researcher introduces herself in Japanese and English.	Students welcome the researcher with applause. They seem to accept her well. They do not show any objection to or irritation at her presence.
00:04:00	Teacher explains the day's tasks, which are about university education in general in Japan and North America.		
00:04:40 00:05:40	Distributes the answer sheets and explains the tasks using the blackboard. Part I: 1) Ask questions; 2) Answer questions; 3) Expand; 4) Feedback; and 5) Disagree politely		Students look at the sheets or chat with their classmates.
00:09:43	Talks about the role of the group leader in order to get options from the whole class.		
00:11:10		One female student sits by herself. Another female student invites her to do the tasks together as a group. She is the group leader for this group, which eventually consists of two female and two male students.	Students move desks and chairs to form groups.
00:16:48 00:17:46	Monitoring and asking questions Teacher does not say anything to her.	One female student comes late for the class and one of the female students tells her what they are doing.	There are seven groups.
00:10:49 00:23:08	Teacher does not say anything to him. Teacher does not say anything to him.	One male student comes late for the class. One male student goes out of the classroom. He comes back at 00:34-58 and rejoins his group, where he resumes.	
00:36:40	Teacher stops the students who are still doing the tasks and asks them to report what they have done.	Each group leader presents a report in turn. 1) How much is the cost? 2) Who makes the payment? 3) What is the age range of the students? 4) How often do the students use the library? Does it open in the evenings or mornings, weekends or Sundays? 5) When does it close? 6) How can students get high marks? 7) How would you describe the teaching style?	

Figure 5.3 **Extract from a classroom observation record (source: Matsumoto 2009).**

Time	Teacher	Individual Students	Groups of students
00:47:55	Part II Suggestion Box: discussion. He writes on the board and explains points of grammar, such as subjunctive sentences: 'If you could…. : 'Why would you change?' 1) Logistical change: classroom conditions, wall. 2) Academic change: credits system, required/optional subjects		The atmosphere within the group becomes friendlier. Students become more communicative, sharing ideas than Part I.
00:53:40	He speaks English at normal speed. Students will discuss two kinds of changes till 11:45 and teacher starts his monitoring.	The Chinese student talks at length with the leader of his groups, obliging the remaining two Japanese students to listen.	Group leaders report back on the discussions in their groups.
01:02:21	He advises going on to the academic suggestions.		The members of this group seem not to understand the meaning of "academic suggestion".
01:14:29	He introduces the sentence, "We would like to suggest when leaders report. Teacher writes what each leader reports on the blackboard.	Each leader reports when the teacher calls his/her name.	Students look at their teacher and listen to him.
01:22:00	Teacher gives his comments.		
01:26:33	He informs the class about the quiz next week and the class is over.		

Figure 5.3 continued

75

Vivian's class: Project on listening comprehension	Charles's class: Project on listening comprehension	Chris's class: Project on listening comprehension	Ange's class: Project on reading comprehension	Carol's class: Project on developing speaking skills
• making connections with previous knowledge • allowing freedom for students to decide groupings • developing/fostering language awareness • showing interest/ allowing students time by themselves but being available for support and feedback • adapting materials to suit students' learning styles • modelling (strategies) • encouraging self-assessment, strategy assessment and assessment of materials > valuing students' opinions	• making connections/ engaging the students' background knowledge • adapting materials to the students' learning styles • developing/fostering language awareness explicitly • prompting and modelling the use of learning strategies, e.g. deduction by using imagery	• adapting materials to suit students' learning styles • developing/ fostering language awareness • praising the students' efforts • modelling (task)	• engaging background knowledge and opinions • modelling (strategy highlighting key words)	• relating topic/ making connections to students' lives • modelling (task in conjunction with a student) • showing interest/ allowing students time by themselves but being available for support and feedback

Figure 5.4 **Comments on teaching practice made by observers in Ormeno's study.**

involved in the activity or becomes a member of the discourse community in order to observe it at close hand. This type of observation is called participant observation. This approach to qualitative data collection will be reviewed in the next section.

Participant observation

Closely associated with (or even coterminous with) ethnographic research, this approach has its origins in anthropology and was originally used to investigate the behaviour and characteristics of particular cultures. This was done by the researcher immersing him or herself totally in the culture under examination, living in the community and using this experience to provide very richly detailed data about how the members of the culture behave on a day-to-day basis.

One applied linguistic study that used participant observation to explore the language used by a particular discourse community is reported in Littlemore et al. (2010). In this study, the aim was to investigate certain features of the language used by staff working in a university nursery. In particular the researchers were interested in the ways in which staff working in the nursery had developed special ways of talking about certain topics which were particular to this discourse community. They were also interested in the contextual factors that had led to the development of these discourse-community-specific meanings and which facilitated their understanding. One of the researchers (Tang) was currently working in the nursery. After having obtained the requisite permission, she wore a microphone every day for work, for two weeks, and another microphone was worn by various different members of staff working in the nursery. Tang was able to collect approximately 20 hours of language spoken by staff in the nursery, which were then transcribed to make a small corpus. This corpus contained a mixture of language used between staff, and by staff when talking to the children. The language used by the children themselves was not transcribed for data protection reasons. The final version of the corpus thus comprised a representative selection of the spoken language used by a particular discourse community, set in the workplace of the university nursery.

In her field notes (i.e. the notes she made during her coffee breaks, while working at the nursery), Tang recorded a figurative usage of 'upstairs' which, for understandable reasons, was not picked up by the tape recorder. This is the use of 'upstairs' to signal a negative evaluation of the senior management team. She notes that the reason why this usage was never recorded was due to the fact that nursery workers usually switched off their microphones when using such language. This reflects one of the weaknesses in this type of research: it is sometimes difficult to obtain recorded data on some of the more sensitive or controversial uses of spoken language in workplace settings. In such cases the researcher needs to rely on field notes – assuming, of course, that he or she is sure that it is appropriate to include such observations in the analysis at all. In noting this point we raise the issue of research ethics, which we will return to this later in this chapter.

There are many issues involved in the collection of spoken data. The researcher may need to choose between using audio recordings and video recordings. The advantage of audio recordings is that they are relatively non-intrusive but there tend to be problems as soon as more than one person is involved if for example, the researcher wants to record conversation in an open-plan office. It can be very difficult to make out who is saying what when one comes to listen to the recording. There are also issues of ethics as the participants must be informed that they are being recorded, but this may seriously affect their behavior as we saw above.

The big disadvantage of audio recordings is that they do not provide any visual information such as the participants' distance from (or proximity to) each other, their facial expressions, or the gestures that they use. Without this information, the researcher only really has part of the picture as far as the communication is concerned. Video recordings provide a fuller picture of the interaction but again raise their own problems. Unless the researcher has access to state of the art recording facilities they will generally only have one camera angle so some of the action may be missed. Video cameras are very intrusive and may well put the participants off the task that they are performing. And they produce gestural data that can be very time-consuming to transcribe. Indeed, even without video data, audio recordings tend to take a long time to transcribe accurately.

On average, most applied linguists would allow ten hours to transcribe each hour of spoken data. Different transcription conventions are used depending on the purpose of the study. Phrases tend to be transcribed using short segments, each of which reflects a single idea (Chafe 1993). Researchers who are interested in investigating the intonation and pitch of the voice need to use supplementary codes to signal pauses, rises in pitch, changes in word stress and so on. It is important to think about what you are planning to do with your data before you start transcribing, so that your transcriptions are done at an appropriate level of detail. Gestures tend to be transcribed at a very detailed level in order to make the studies replicable. A good account of gesture transcription conventions can be found in Bressem (2008).

Triangulation

Like many qualitative studies in applied linguistics, the nursery study discussed above is to some extent *triangulated*. That is to say, the same issue is investigated using a variety of research techniques, each of which shows it in a different light and complements the findings obtained by the other approaches. The main data collection activity was the recording work done by the participant observer, but this was complemented by a questionnaire, Tang's field notes, and a computerised corpus analysis. The advantage of triangulating data in this way is that it reduces the probability that the particular data collection technique that one has chosen will highlight some aspects of the data while downplaying others. Data triangulation helps researchers to get a much more rounded view of the phenomena that they are interested in.

Another example of triangulation can be seen in Matsumoto's (2009) study of Japanese university EFL classrooms. By combining classroom observation with interviews with both teachers and students and questionnaires, Matsumoto was able to obtain a fuller picture of the classroom dynamics as seen from the students', the teachers' and the observer's own perspectives. One feature of Matsumoto's data that shed quite a lot of light on other pieces of data was her diagrams of the seating arrangements and teachers' movements in each of the classrooms that she studied. By looking at these it was possible to see at a glance which classrooms were (at least superficially) more communicative and which were more 'traditional'. An example of one of these diagrams is shown in Figure 5.5.

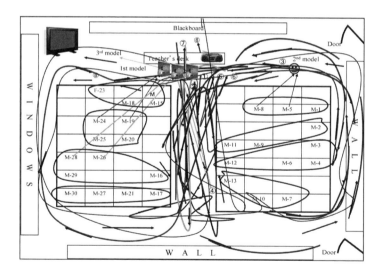

Figure 5.5 Teacher's movement and seating arrangements in one of the classes observed by Matsumoto (2009).

In Matsumoto's study, each of these diagrams is followed by a detailed description of what went on in the class on a minute-by-minute basis. Matsumoto was able to use these to compare different types of interaction and dynamics in different classes. She also used them as a basis for the interviews that she later conducted with both the teacher and some of the students about how they had viewed the different types of interaction that had taken place during the class.

Research ethics in qualitative data collection

Because qualitative research is often highly personal, and in some cases potentially even intrusive, researchers need to attend particularly carefully to the ethical implications of their research. As with quantitative research, (which we will discuss in detail in Chapters 7 and 8), it is important to get the participants' permission and to make them aware of the aims of the study. However, unlike quantitative research, anonymity is not always possible, or even desirable in qualitative research. In Myers' study of the two research scientists mentioned above, the real names of the scientists are actually provided along with a great deal of personal background information. Participants in such a study need to be very clear about what exactly will appear in the final research report or article, and if possible given a copy of the article to read and approve or amend before it is published.

Of all the examples of research mentioned above, the study that involved data collection in a nursery is clearly the most sensitive. Not only was it necessary to remove all names from the transcript data, but the researchers also had to delete all of the children's utterances, as permission to collect, store and analyse these data had not been obtained. Permission had to be obtained from all members of staff who might have been recorded and if any had objected (in this case they did not) then the microphone would have needed to be switched off in their presence. When asking for permission, it was also necessary to make the nursery staff aware of the overall aims of the study (to investigate the language used by staff working in the nursery) without jeopardising the results of the study. For example, if they had been told that the focus would be on figurative language, this may have increased or decreased the amount of figurative language produced. It is also standard practice for a researcher to give her or his 'research subjects' the opportunity to see the results of the research and to delete anything that they are not happy with. As with quantitative research, a full set of guidelines for good practice in qualitative research in applied linguistics is provided by the British Association for Applied Linguistics (www.baal.org.uk).

Conclusion

There are many different ways of collecting qualitative data, and researchers will often combine two or more approaches in the same study so that the same phenomenon can be explored from different angles. In this chapter we have looked at some of the most widely-used qualitative data gathering techniques in applied linguistics, namely: interviews, introspective techniques, case studies and observation. In the next chapter we will move on to consider some of the ways in which researchers go about analysing qualitative data once they have finished collecting it – or, in some cases, while they are still collecting it.

6

Analysing qualitative data

Introduction

In Chapter 5 we looked at some of the different ways in which qualitative data can be collected in applied linguistics. In this chapter we look at what applied linguists do with such data once they have collected it. In other words, we look at how they analyse qualitative data so that they can use it to answer specific research questions. The chapter will be organised around two fundamental perspectives on the analysis of qualitative data. In applied linguistics (and in the humanities and social sciences more generally) these are often referred to as *etic* and *emic* perspectives. The etic perspective looks at qualitative data 'from the outside', as it were, by identifying patterns and regularities that may not be visible to the participants in the research themselves. In direct contrast, the emic perspective attempts to view qualitative data 'from the inside', by capturing participants' own understandings of what is going on, or at least interpreting qualitative data in ways that the participants might recognise and accept as being consistent with their own perspectives on events. Etic analysis always involves some form of data categorisation, so we will begin by discussing what this is and how it is done. We will then look in detail at conversation analysis, which is arguably the most rigorous (and certainly the most popular) of the currently available approaches to emic analysis in applied linguistics.

The etic perspective: categorisation

For the vast majority of the time, we all go about our everyday lives without thinking consciously about what we are doing, or how or why we are doing it. To borrow a famous advertising slogan, we 'just do it', and – most of the time – it works for us. Indeed, one of the main reasons why we do not think about what we are doing is precisely *because* it works for us. We do not *need* to think about it. When we (the authors of this book) greet our work colleagues each day we do not usually need to think about what to say, how to say it or whether to say it; it comes as naturally to us as breathing to say "Morning", "Hi" or whatever happens to be appropriate at that particular point in time. Nor do we need to think in a more abstract way about what we are doing when we say "Morning" or "Hi" to our colleagues. We do not say (nor do we need to say) to ourselves 'Aha! Here I am greeting a colleague!' or 'Aha! In greeting my colleague I am actively working to maintain good relations with this colleague', even if we have recently upset this colleague and are now greeting them in a bid to re-establish good relations with them. We just do it.

At a very basic level, it is possible to say that the whole purpose of qualitative research is to engage in precisely this kind of questioning: to reflect consciously on the things that we normally never reflect consciously on. One of the most popular ways of doing this in applied linguistics is to categorise each instance of a particular action, using a labelling term that you have formulated yourself, or which is already available as a common-sense descriptor or has been developed by previous researchers. In our simple illustrative example above, we could categorise "Morning" and "Hi" in two ways, each of which represents a different level of abstraction. At one level of abstraction we can categorise these utterances as instances of the functional category 'Greeting'. At another, higher, level of abstraction, we can categorise them (together with any other utterances falling into the 'Greeting' category in our data) as instances of a category that we could call 'Bonding'. This broader and more abstract category will also contain other kinds of utterance, which have already been put into other kinds of functional subcategory. For example, 'Bonding' may also contain utterances such as 'Have a great weekend' or 'See you next week', which we may have labelled at our lower level of theoretical abstraction as instances of the functional category 'Closing'.

While 'Greeting' and 'Closing' are clearly categories based on linguistic functions, you may be wondering what 'Bonding' is a category of. One answer to this question is provided by a study by Ädel (2010), who proposes that it is a manifestation of the basic human need to maintain positive relations with others in the various social groups to which they belong. Drawing on previous research in applied linguistics, Ädel gives this even more abstract and general level of analysis the category label *rapport building*. In her own research, Ädel was interested in studying and comparing rapport building among two groups of university students: campus-based students working in face-to-face interactions in university seminars and distance students working on collaborative tasks together via the 'discussion forum' section of an online Virtual Learning Environment (VLE). As well as observing many examples of 'Greeting' and 'Closing', Ädel also identified a further thirteen functional categories in her data, which she divided into four higher-level groups. A summary of Ädel's analytical scheme is provided in Table 6.1.

As can be seen, 'Bonding' is by far the largest category of rapport building in functional terms. This does not necessarily mean that 'Bonding' utterances occur more frequently in Ädel's data than the other types listed above do, however. In this study, Ädel was interested only in mapping out the different kinds of function that occurred in the data that she studied, and she did not attempt to quantify each kind or establish their relative proportions. One very significant quantitative observation that Ädel does mention, however, is that two of the categories above, 'Excusing oneself' and 'Phatic communication', were only found to occur in the face-to-face student data. The absence in the distance learning data of instances of students excusing themselves in order to take a short break is easy enough to explain. The distance students are not physically co-present (i.e. located together in the same place at the same point in time), and they are working on their tasks asynchronously (i.e. the courses that they are taking do not require them to log into the VLE and work on their tasks together at the same time). In such a context, it is entirely unnecessary to post a message to your fellow group members announcing that you are going to get yourself a coffee, and that you will be back in five minutes. The face-to-face interactions, in contrast, are happening in real time and are being conducted by students who are physically co-present. In this latter context, it is normal in the country where the face-to-face data were collected (the USA) for a member of a group to announce to the other members of that group that they need

Table 6.1 **Categories of rapport building among university students.**

Type of unit	Function	Example
Bonding	Agreeing	*Yeah, I agree*
	Aligning with in-group	*I also found myself unsure on 2L*
	Commiserating	*Just like you I would appreciate a key for the old exam*
	Complimenting	*You guys are brilliant*
	Offering encouragement	*Great job!!!!!!*
	Phatic communication (off task)	*Gonna watch the M-S-U game tonight?*
	Responding to thanks	*You're welcome*
	Seeking agreement	*You know what I'm saying?*
	Thanking	*Thank you!*
Message-structuring	Greeting	*Hi there*
	Closing	*Have a good weekend*
	Excusing oneself	*I'll be right back*
Face-saving	Apologising	*I'm sorry i don't know why I'm so retarded*
	Mitigating criticism	*Just have some small comments to your answers, hopefully it might be useful*
Inter-textual	Referring to in-group discourse	*You know how we talked about how, single fathers, who…*

Source: adapted from Ädel 2010.

to break off temporarily from an activity that is currently in progress, and to reassure the other members of the group explicitly or implicitly that they will return shortly and rejoin the task activity. Failure to do this would almost certainly leave the other members of the group wondering whether the individual concerned was angry or offended about something, or whether this person is simply behaving in a lazy, selfish or inconsiderate way. Note also that this would not be true of all cultures. Indeed, in some cultures it would be entirely normal for an individual to leave a group activity and then rejoin it shortly afterwards without saying anything at all. In such a cultural context, making some kind of explicit statement of intent or explanation in this regard might well be regarded as odd, inappropriate, embarrassing or even insulting to the other group members.

The absence of any instances of 'Phatic communication' is more intriguing, however. 'Phatic communication' in Ädel's research means small talk unrelated to the task at hand. In her face-to-face data, Ädel found that students engaged in a lot of such talk: so much so, in fact, that she was able to divide it into a series of topic-based subcategories of its own: 'Weather' (e.g. *I can't believe it's so warm out right now*), 'Health and wellbeing' (*I'm starting to come down with something*), 'Leisure' (*gonna watch the M-S-U game tonight?*) and 'Food' (*I need a coffee*). Although some of these kinds of utterance clearly relate to the strictly here-and-now, there is no particular reason why distance students working asynchronously in a VLE cannot engage in some form of small talk, and yet the students in Ädel's study did not. Does the absence of phatic communication in the distance student data mean that their learning experience is in some way impoverished compared to that of their campus-based peers? If so, then Ädel's research has clear implications for university teachers and researchers in the field of higher education studies. If on the other hand it can be shown that the distance students are able to complete group tasks just as well as their campus-based peers do, then Ädel's research raises the question of whether phatic communication is as important as many previous researchers have assumed it to be. In this sense, Ädel's research is an excellent example of what applied linguistic research is uniquely able to do: it raises questions for academic theorists, for language professionals and for lay people engaged in particular real-world practices, all at the same time.

Before concluding this section, there is one very important caveat that we want to express about categorisation as an approach to the empirical analysis of qualitative data in applied linguistics: it is nowhere near as easy as it looks! The neat system of categories and subcategories that Ädel generated in her research may seem very clear-cut and self-evident as they are presented in Table 6.1, but it is only possible to arrive at such a system after a long and sometimes arduous process of engagement with the raw data itself. During this process, categories will be created, refined, merged, split and sometimes discarded altogether if it subsequently becomes clear that they are irrelevant or do not adequately fit the data that you are interested in. This inevitably raises the question of when the process of categorisation is finished. In principle, the answer to this question is 'never': a system of categories can always be revised and refined ad infinitum as it encounters fresh data. In practice, however, you will find that as you continue to test your system on fresh data it will begin to 'stabilise'. That is, you will need to make fewer and fewer changes to your model, and the changes that you need to make will become progressively smaller and more fine-grained. Eventually you will arrive at a point where you either no longer need to generate any new categories at all, or where the model you are developing is stable enough for your own particular research purposes. Nevertheless, it is important to keep in mind that categories in qualitative (and, indeed, in quantitative) data are not unproblematic reflections of reality. On the contrary, categories are ad hoc creations that emerge from a particular research context, are susceptible to change, and have fuzzy boundaries.

Towards an emic perspective: conversation analysis

One of the problems with ascribing categories to qualitative data in an applied linguistics research project is that the people involved in the study may not actually define themselves in those ways. For example, researchers might use linguistic criteria to establish categories of conservative and moderate religious believers, but the participants in their studies may not recognise these terms as valid ways of conceptualising their beliefs. Also, most people belong to a range of different social groups and are often able (and indeed are sometimes required) to shift identities to a greater or lesser degree as they live their daily lives, so the allocation of human behaviour to fixed, rigid categories is thus inevitably an artificial and reductive activity. Finally, some qualitative researchers have criticised category-based research of the kind we have been discussing so far on the grounds that it requires researchers to assume that a phenomenon actually exists before they find any empirical evidence of it in their own data. In this sense, category-based research imposes meanings and values on data, rather than allowing meanings and values to emerge from the data during the process of analysis itself.

One approach that attempts to resolve this latter problem is *grounded theory*. In this approach, the researcher starts off with no preconceptions at all about the data. The coding process then consists of three stages. In the first stage, open coding, the researcher divides the transcript into utterances. He or she then looks at every utterance and decides what it means, what it might an example of, and what principles might underlie it. By doing so, he or she is able to establish a number of preliminary categories. Having done this, he or she then moves to stage two, axial coding, in which he or she identifies links between the categories established in stage one. After this has been done, he or she proceeds to stage three, selective coding, which involves the identification of a 'core category' around which all the others will sit. This core category will then form the centrepiece of the study.

A more radical way of dealing with the problem of imposing external categories on the communicative practices of individuals and groups is to attempt to avoid imposing external categories altogether, and to attempt instead to develop a perspective that reflects how the participants in an event or situation understand what they are doing, and what is going on around them. The most commonly used approach in applied linguistics that explicitly tries to present such an emic view is known as conversation analysis.

As the name suggests, conversation analysis (henceforth CA) was originally developed as an approach to the analysis of informal spoken language, but it is not a linguistic framework as such – it is derived from ethnomethodology (a branch of sociology), and is interested in the content of talk not the language. However, CA has long been very popular among applied linguists, and in fact is a good example of how applied linguists have appropriated theoretical and methodological frameworks from outside linguistics.

CA attempts to be true to the emic perspective by adhering to a strict set of tenets and procedures. Central among these is the practice of what conversation analysts call unmotivated looking. Essentially, this means studying a transcript completely inductively, which is to say, without having any prior conception of what might be found within it. In a CA study there can be no hunting for particular features such as we saw earlier in the example of Ädel's study of rapport building language. Neither is the analyst allowed to compare what is going on in a particular situation with what people usually do in this situation, or even to known contextual features that are not actually mentioned in transcript. The only features of context that conversation analysts allow themselves to take into account are those that the participants themselves explicitly 'orient themselves' towards in their talk. Because of this exclusive focus on the explicit 'here-and-now' of a given interaction, conversation analysts tend to transcribe their data in great detail. To illustrate, consider the transcript in Figure 6.1 and the key that follows it. Both are taken from a study of business interactions conducted by Koester (2004). This extract features two speakers: Jim, a university professor, and Liz, a secretary in the same department.

1. Jim   I was wondering if… you an' I could *possibly*
         this week, at about eleven o'clock on Thursday
         morning, *reinforce* each other half an hour on-
         just to look through [name of journal] and see
         where we are.
2. Liz   ⌊Yes. ⌊it's- it's on my mind *terribly*, in fact →
3. Jim   ⌊yeah
4. Liz   I've been dreaming about it all night.
5. Jim   Well I had a dream about it as *well*.
6. Liz   ⌊So-
7. Liz   I've got to get i- because it's on my mind so much
         I-
8. Jim   ⌊It's funny   ⌊a
         really guilty conscience about it =
9. Liz   = Yes, I am, so I *must* … get on and do it.
10. Liz   So yes, Thursday at eleven will be fine.

.	falling intonation
…	noticeable pause or break of less than 1 second within a turn
-	sound abruptly cut off, e.g., false start
italics	emphatic stress
→	speaker's turn continues without interruption
⌊	overlapping or simultaneous speech
=	latching: no perceptible inter-turn pause
[ ]	words in these brackets indicate non-linguistic information, e.g. pauses of 1 second or longer (the number of seconds is indicated), speakers' gestures or actions.

Figure 6.1 **Transcription conventions used by Koester (2004).**

From a CA perspective, there are a number of observations that can be made about this extract. First of all, and as can be seen, the main purpose of this interaction is to arrange a meeting. Specifically, Jim asks Liz to meet with him in order to work on an academic journal that he edits, and Liz accepts. This 'Invitation – Accept' sequence is very common in all forms of conversational interaction, and is an example of what conversation analysts call an adjacency pair. The concept of adjacency pair was coined in recognition of the fact that, while all conversations are essentially just sequences of speaker turns, some types of turn are more likely to go together than others. Other common adjacency pairs identified by conversation analysts include 'Greeting – Greeting' and 'Question – Answer'.

Second, we may note that this adjacency pair is not particularly adjacent: the invitation occurs in Line 1, but the acceptance does not come until line 10. In between the two pair parts there is a fairly lengthy side sequence, in which Jim and Liz discuss their guilty feelings about having neglected this work recently. Again, conversation analysts have established that such sequences are a very common feature of everyday talk. Here is another (and shorter) authentic example, recorded by one of the authors of this book during a recent visit to a coffee bar:

Customer:	Small cappuccino, please.
Barista:	Regular or free trade?
Customer:	Er free trade.
Barista:	OK.

However, conversation analysts are much less interested in identifying structural patterns such as this than they are in asking *how and why people are using them* in particular interactions. With regard to the extract above, Koester (2004: 1419) suggests that

> The function of this side sequence seems to be for the participants to demonstrate how urgent they both feel the proposed meeting is. Thus, prior to responding to Jim's proposal, Liz demonstrates in turn 2 ('it's on my mind terribly') that she has understood something implied in his initial utterance, which is not obvious from the actual wording: the urgency of the meeting.

Koester finds that sequences such as this are very common in workplace interactions. She terms them 'relational sequences', on the grounds that they are primarily geared towards interpersonal relationships and are not essential for getting the job done. The prevalence of these sequences, and their intermingling with turn-taking sequences of a more transactional nature, lead Koester to argue that there is no clear-cut distinction between 'institutional talk' and 'ordinary conversation' in the workplace. Whereas business communication is often seen (and taught) in entirely transactional terms, Koester's analysis shows that a lot of workplace talk is actually interactional. This can clearly be seen in the extract above, where the two speakers spend more time talking about their own psychological states than they do about the working arrangement that they are supposed to be making.

A current controversy among qualitative researchers in applied linguistics concerns the status of the theoretical concepts and generalisations (such as turn-taking, adjacency pairs and side sequences) that have arisen out of CA research over the last few decades. For some researchers it is a fundamental mistake to regard the observations arising from CA as an intrinsic part of its method. The applied linguist and conversational analyst Paul Seedhouse (an example of whose own work we will consider in detail in Chapter 9) claims that much CA in applied linguistics is not 'true' CA but 'linguistic CA', which he regards as a problematic dilution of CA as an approach to the study of social interaction:

> Linguistic CA is basically CA minus the methodology: a kind of coding scheme. Metaphorically, it presents the reader with a Porsche which has had a lawn mower engine installed in it. It may have the same name, badge, and bodywork as a normal Porsche and crawl forward in the same direction after a fashion, but the power is no longer there.

> (Seedhouse 2004: 51)

Meanwhile, some other analysts have criticised CA for what they see as its obstinate and ultimately self-defeating refusal to make more systematic use of the insights gained from its own analyses. CA has also been criticised for being indifferent to the broader social situations that exist behind particular instances of talk-as-interaction, particularly where there are unequal power relations between participants. These caveats notwithstanding, it remains the case that CA offers perhaps the most powerful set of methodological tools for applied linguists who wish to research a particular problem, question or issue from an emic perspective, that is to say, in a way that tries to see things from the point of view of the people involved in that particular problem, question or issue themselves. If you are interested in finding out more about CA, the detailed accounts provided by ten Have (2007), Richards and Seedhouse (2007) and Hutchby and Wooffit (2008) provide excellent starting points.

Conclusion

In this chapter we have looked at the two main ways in which applied linguists analyse qualitative data. We have seen that they can either adopt an etic perspective, by analysing data into categories developed by themselves or by previous researchers, or they can adopt an emic perspective, in an attempt to identify and understand how the participants in the data interpret what is going on in a given situation. We have also pointed out some of the limitations of each of these broad orientations to qualitative research, and sketched out a few of the major criticisms of each.

As we have seen, qualitative research is primarily interested in establishing *what* things happen, *how* things happen, and *why* things happen in particular real-world situations. However, once you have established a system for categorising different forms of rapport building language, or established that relational side sequences can occur within transactional exchanges in workplace interactions, it becomes possible to ask *how often* these things happen, too. In other words, it becomes possible to conduct a study of a more *quantitative* nature. The next two chapters will focus on some of the main ways in which quantitative research in applied linguistics is carried out.

7

Collecting
quantitative data

Introduction

In this chapter we begin to look at how quantitative data are used to answer particular kinds of research question in applied linguistics. The chapter begins by considering the nature of quantitative data, and how these data differ in fundamental ways from the qualitative forms of data discussed in the previous two chapters. We then look at issues of sampling and data collection through questionnaires and other tools, and illustrate our points by referring to studies in applied linguistics that have needed to address these issues. By the end of this chapter, you should know enough about collecting quantitative data to understand how and why applied linguists go about collecting such data. You should also be in a good position to start planning the data collection stage of a small quantitative applied linguistic study of your own.

The nature of quantitative data

Whereas qualitative data provide the researcher with in-depth detailed knowledge of a particular phenomenon, quantitative data tend to provide a broad-brush overview of general trends and relationships. They can tell us, for example, that there are overall differences between groups of people in terms of their linguistic behaviour and/or ability but they tell us very little about the individuals within our study. Quantitative data can be very useful in analysing things such as the overall benefits of particular language policy or of a particular teaching approach, but care should be taken to counterbalance them with qualitative data as they only ever provide a partial, largely superficial picture of reality. With this caveat in mind, we now turn to the details of quantitative data collection.

Choosing a representative sample

When applied linguists collect quantitative data they usually carry out their research on a particular sample of language users or learners, and try to extrapolate from their findings to make claims about language users or learners more generally. However, it is important to bear in mind that whatever findings we obtain in our research only *really* apply to the particular group of people studied, at the time they were studied, and in the particular circumstances in which they were studied. For example, Derwing *et al.* (2007) carried out a study comparing the development of oral fluency of 32 well-educated adult immigrants from Mandarin and Slavic language backgrounds enrolled in introductory English as a second language (ESL) classes in Canada. They found that the Slavic language speakers made a small but significant improvement in both fluency and comprehensibility, whereas the Mandarin speakers' performance did not change over two years, despite the fact that both groups started at the same level of oral proficiency. It would be inappropriate to claim, on the basis of these results, that *all* Slavic language speakers are better at learning English than *all* Mandarin speakers. The study has only shown that *these particular learners* happened to make more improvements in *oral fluency* (not other aspects of language learning) in this particular context. We can attempt to extrapolate from the sample studied but this carries a degree of risk (which we will explore in more depth in Chapter 8).

This issue of context-dependency applies to all applied linguistics research, whether it be qualitative, quantitative or a mixture of the two. However, there are measures that we can take in our research design that allow us to generalise beyond the group of participants with whom we conducted our study. In order to assess the generalisability of our findings, we need to consider three factors:

- Our target population
- Our sample
- The representativeness of that sample

The target population refers to the group of people that we want to make a claim about. In the Derwing *et al.* study, the target population appears to be 'adult immigrant learners of English in Canada'. The findings of the study are used to make a set of recommendations about how these particular learners might be offered further support through their programmes. No claims are made about 'language learners in general' and no recommendations are made at this level. The sample of learners chosen for the study consists of 32 learners who fall into this category and is therefore representative of the target population as a whole. The issue of representativeness is important in sample selection. If we say that a sample is representative of a particular target population, we are saying that the sample is a kind of smaller, 'mini' version of that target population. There are several ways of making a sample more representative of the target population. One is to make it as large as possible. The closer the sample is in size to the target population, the more reliable predictor it is likely to be of the behaviour of that population as a whole.

The optimum sample size will depend partly on the type of study we are conducting. The sample size in the Derwing *et al.* study (N=32) is rather small for a quantitative study, but the researchers also carried out some extensive qualitative research (for example, the students were interviewed and asked to complete questionnaires) so for this study, a smaller number of participants was more practical. For a more purely quantitative study a larger number of participants would have been appropriate. Normally, for a quantitative study that aims to make comparisons between two groups of people, one would expect to have a minimum of 30 participants in each group, giving a total of 60 participants. If however, we wanted to investigate statistical relationships between a large number of variables, we would need a much larger group. So if Derwing *et al.* had also wanted to make a statistical analysis of, say, the effects of their participants' attitudes to Canadian culture, desire to live in Canada, degree of open mindedness and levels of motivation on their degree of fluency and comprehensibility, they would have needed to use a very large sample indeed (at least 200 in this case) as there would be so many variables in the study. The term 'variables' simply means 'things that we are looking at and attempting to measure' so it could include a wide range of phenomena, such as 'speaking ability', 'test performance', 'level of motivation', 'attitude to the target language culture', and so on.

Besides having a large enough sample, there are other ways of ensuring that the sample we use is representative of our target population. One way is to use a robust sampling technique. There are many different ways of collecting samples, some of which are better than others. Here are a few of the main ones, presented in order of reliability.

The most robust and reliable form of sampling is random sampling. If Derwing *et al.* had managed to find ESL students with Mandarin and Slavic linguistic backgrounds from all over Canada and from a range of different language programmes, this would have been a true 'random sample'. However, true random sampling such as this is very rare if not non-existent in applied linguistics. It is very unlikely that a researcher will ever be in a situation where he or she is able to select participants *completely* randomly. In the Derwing *et al.* study, all the participants were studying on the same programme, at the same institution and living in the same town, so the sampling was not random. Like many researchers, Derwing *et al.* selected their sample from people to whom they had access. However, as we will see below, this is not a problem as they were able to provide a strong justification for their particular choice of subjects.

Another type of sampling is systematic sampling. In the context of a classroom research project, this might involve choosing, say, every fifth student on the class register. Although this is not entirely random (as it is based on a single class), the choice of every fifth student prevents subjectivity on the part of the researcher. Related to systematic sampling is stratified random sampling. Here for example, a researcher might study ten students at beginner's level, ten lower-intermediate students, ten intermediate, ten upper-intermediate and ten advanced students. This would lead to a reasonable range of participants spread fairly evenly across the different levels. Another sampling technique that increases the degree of randomness is quota sampling. This involves getting similar numbers of different types of participants, but there is no hierarchy involved. If an investigator doesn't want the results to be gender specific, he or she might include ten male students and ten female students in the study.

Many applied linguistic researchers find themselves in a position where they need to use opportunity sampling. This involves conducting the research with whatever participants happen to be available. This appears to be the sampling strategy adopted by Derwing *et al.*, as the students in their study were all attending a college in Edmonton, the city where one of the researchers was working. There is nothing wrong with this sort of sampling. In fact it can be beneficial in many ways as the researcher is more likely to be familiar with the social context and the living conditions of the participants in the study. In this particular study, which also contains a strong qualitative element including reflections on how the two immigrant groups are treated by Canadian citizens, this kind of background knowledge is essential. The important thing in this study, as far as sampling is concerned, is that the students in the two groups were matched as far as possible in terms of their stage of learning, levels of proficiency and gender.

A type of sampling that is often used by applied linguistics students is snowball sampling. Here, for example, a researcher may want to find out the main language difficulties faced by international students studying at his or her university so he or she emails a questionnaire to a few close friends and asks them to forward it to anyone they know who might be interested. The group of people involved in the study therefore gets bigger and bigger as it goes along in a fairly random manner, hence the 'snowball' analogy. At times it is the only form of sampling possible. The important thing when reading or doing applied linguistics is to be aware of the nature of the sample studied and of the restrictions that this places on the extent to which the findings can be extrapolated to other individuals.

Before leaving this subject, we would like to mention a number of other issues that need to be considered when selecting a sample. One is that the researcher will often need to control for unwanted variables. For example, in a recent study, one of the authors (Littlemore 2001) was interested in looking at the relationship between learning styles and strategy preferences in language learners. The study included learners of both Spanish and Japanese and was therefore not controlled for language of study. The results showed a huge, statistically significant difference in terms of the language being studied, and thus ended up saying more about the strategy preferences of learners of different languages, than about the relationship between styles and strategy preferences per se. Other variables that one might need to control for include gender, age, L1 background, and level.

A final issue to consider is the problem of self-selection – if a researcher asks for volunteers he or she may end up with a sample of 'extra keen' participants who are not typical of most students. Equally, if the study involves optional completion of a questionnaire, the researcher needs to ensure that he or she has replies from a wide range of students, not just the willing ones. And finally, the researcher needs to allow for a wide margin of error. Unless one has a captive audience, survey response rates tend to hover round the 20 per cent rate, and of these a fair number of participants will misread the instructions or interpret the questions in ways that the researcher has not predicted. For these reasons, it is often a good idea to pilot one's research with a small group of respondents. This will allow the researcher to iron out any difficulties before moving on to the main study.

Conducting questionnaire research

A significant amount of applied linguistics research involves the use of questionnaires, and in this section we outline some of the most important 'dos and don'ts' in questionnaire design. Our account is not exhaustive, however, and for a fully comprehensive review of the use of questionnaires in applied linguistic research we strongly recommend Dörnyei's (2003) *Questionnaires in Second Language Research: Construction, Administration, and Processing*. When designing a questionnaire, the researcher needs to bear in mind that it will never provide direct information about people's behaviour. It will only provide information about what they think about their behaviour. This is one of the problems inherent in self-report data. Borg and Burns (2008) provide an interesting way of overcoming this problem. They were interested in exploring teachers' beliefs about the role of grammar in the language classroom. They administered a lengthy 'beliefs' questionnaire to over 176 English language teachers from 18 countries in order to get an overview of the views that these teachers held. One of their questions was as follows:

1a   In your teaching, to what extent is grammar teaching integrated with the teaching of other skills? (Tick ONE)

No integration ☐	Some integration ☐	Substantial integration ☐	Complete integration ☐

This is the sort of question that respondents may not have been able to answer well initially, due to a possible lack of insight into their own behaviour. In order to mitigate this potential problem, Borg and Burns added a 'part b', which forced their respondents to illustrate their response and thus to think more deeply about the question:

1b   Please explain your answer to 1a by describing the relationship between grammar teaching and the teaching of language skills (reading, writing, speaking, listening) in your lessons.

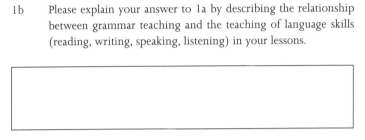

Other potential problems with questionnaires include the fact that when completing questionnaires, people sometimes try to write what they think the researcher wants to hear, rather than what they actually think. This is known as positive response bias. Also, questionnaires sometimes provide inaccurate information about what people really think. This issue can be explored by asking respondents what they meant when they gave a particular answer to an item on a questionnaire. Sometimes researchers will get as many different answers to this follow-up question as there are participants, even if the participants' answers on the questionnaire are identical. In short, questionnaire data will only ever give you a superficial view of the phenomenon you are interested in. To get in-depth answers it is necessary to use interview techniques, classroom observations or other types of data triangulation (see Chapter 5).

Sometimes when writing a questionnaire there is a temptation to add lots of demographic questions about the participant's name, age, background and so on. But is this always really necessary? There are two issues that need to be borne in mind here. The first is the issue of anonymity. If a language teacher is administering a questionnaire to his or her own students and then asks them to provide their names, the students may get the impression that their answers to the questionnaire will influence the teacher's impression of them or even the grades that they will be awarded at the end of term. If this is the case, then the teacher-researcher may need to make the questionnaire anonymous. This may be difficult however if they then want to compare the questionnaire data with the students' performance on the test, and need to match the pieces of data that come from the same person. One solution here is to ask the participants to use a code name or number and to use the same code name or number in the second part of the study. This allows the researcher to match the pieces of data without knowing who the participant is.

The second problem with asking for lots of biographical information is that the respondents may easily tire of having to answer too many questions. If there is no direct benefit to the participants from filling in the questionnaire, the researcher needs to find some guarantee that they will fill it in conscientiously and accurately. One way to increase the chances of them taking it seriously is for the researcher not to make it too long. The questionnaire administered by Borg and Burns asks only for the background information that is relevant to the study. This includes details of the participant's years of experience, teaching qualifications and teaching situation. It does not ask for their name or age.

Another thing to bear in mind when administering a questionnaire is the setting, and even the timing, of the administration. A questionnaire completed in class may elicit very different answers from a questionnaire completed in the participants' own time at home. When the respondent is completing a questionnaire at home in his or her own time he or she will have access to a wider variety of resources, reference books and so on, and may thus provide more considered responses to the questions. However the rate of return of the questionnaires is likely to be much lower than it would be if they were given out in class and the respondents given a certain amount of time to complete them. The key consideration is to make sure that all the respondents fill out the questionnaire and are completing the questionnaire in roughly the same conditions as each other. This may even include the time of day or the time of year. The attitudes that a group of teachers holds towards their profession may be very different on the Monday morning at the start of term from those held on a Friday afternoon just before they break up for their long vacation.

Before administering a questionnaire it is important to make it clear to the participants what is going to be done with the findings. Are they going to be shared with any other researchers? Are they going to be published with their names on? Are they going to be shown to other teachers? It is important that the participants understand the full consequences of being involved in the study, so that they can then give their informed consent. A set of useful guidelines on the issue of informed consent and other research ethics in applied linguistics can be found on the website of the British Association for Applied Linguistics (www.baal.org.uk).

As mentioned earlier, before conducting any study involving a questionnaire it is very important to pilot the questionnaire itself. In other words, the questionnaire needs to be tested out on a smaller group of participants who are similar to, but not the same as, those with whom you plan to conduct the main study. This will provide information about any items that are badly worded or confusing, and will give an indication of the amount of time needed to fill in the questionnaire. After the pilot session it is worth discussing with the participants any problems that they perceived with your questionnaire or its administration. These can then be put right in time for the main study. The researcher also needs to make sure that none of the people involved in the pilot study are subsequently involved in the main study. The questionnaire in Borg and Burns' study was piloted on 23 teachers in two different countries.

When putting together a questionnaire, it is also important to think about the different question types that will be used. The two main types are open-ended questions, or fixed-response questions. In open-ended questions, there is no control over what the respondent writes. These might include questions such as:

What is/are your main reason(s) for wanting to learn English?

or sentences that need to be completed, such as:

My main reasons for learning English are …

One thing to consider when writing a questionnaire is the issue of whether you put open-ended questions at the beginning or the end of the questionnaire. The advantage of putting them at the beginning is that the respondents have not yet got bored by your questionnaire so are arguably more likely to answer them fully. Also, open-ended questions might get them into a deep-thinking frame of mind which will be useful when they are completing the rest of the questionnaire. On the other hand some open-ended questions may skew their responses to future questions.

The other type of question is the fixed-response question. Here the respondent has to select from a series of answers that have been pre-selected by the researcher. The Borg and Burns questionnaire contains fixed response questions, such as the following:

Which ONE of the following best describes the status of English for your adult learners?

English as a foreign language	English as a second language
☐	☐

One of the problems with fixed-response questions is that the answers have been pre-selected by the researcher so the respondent is forced to choose between a set of options that may not correspond closely to his or her own thoughts. For example, the two questions above presuppose that there is a clear distinction between 'English as a foreign language' (which usually refers to teaching situations where the student is not resident in the target language community) and 'English as a second language' (which usually refers to teaching situations where the student is resident in the target language community). Many language teaching situations are a hybrid of the two. This is not a problem for the Borg and Burns study as their aim was to ensure that they collected data from both types of teaching situations. However if the aim of their study had been to compare the two situations, they would have needed to further refine this questionnaire item. Researchers sometimes use an 'other' box to get round this problem, but this raises its own set of problems as it can be difficult to systematically analyse what is written in the 'other' box. This type of question exemplifies a widespread dilemma in social science research: the trade-off between a desire to collect data that can be analysed statistically and then generalised to a wider population, and the need to get accurate in-depth data about what people actually think. One way to overcome this dilemma is to employ a mixed-methods mode of research which combines large quantities of 'objective' quantitative data with data from smaller, more focused in-depth qualitative studies.

Another common form of fixed-response question is the Likert Scale. An example of one of these is shown in Figure 7.1.

For each of the following items, circle a number from 1 to 5, where:

1 = strongly disagree
2 = disagree to some extent
3 = neither agree nor disagree
4 = agree to some extent
5 = strongly agree

1.	The teacher should try to correct all errors that are made by students.	1	2	3	4	5
2.	The teacher should only correct errors that relate to the specific language points taught in a particular lesson.	1	2	3	4	5
3.	The teacher should focus on grammar when listening to his or her students.	1	2	3	4	5

Figure 7.1 **An example of a Likert Scale.**

When designing Likert Scale questions there are a number of things to bear in mind. First, you must include items that are easy to understand. You should avoid questions that contain two parts as it will not always be clear to the participants which part they should answer. For example, in the following question:

> *Learning a new language can be difficult and I like it that way.*

Participants may be unsure as to whether they are supposed to agree with the statement that 'learning a new language can be difficult' or with the statement that 'they like it that way'. It is also important to avoid items that contain double negatives as these can be very confusing. For example if participants are asked whether or not they agree with the statement:

> *I don't like it when the teacher doesn't tell me what I have done wrong.*

they may easily miss one of the negatives and perceive the statement to be either 'I don't like it when the teacher tells me what I have done wrong' or 'I like it when the teacher doesn't tell me what I have done wrong'. Another type of item to be avoided, and which can easily be identified during the piloting stage, is the type of item that is likely to be answered in the same way by everyone in the study. For example the following item:

I like it when the teacher makes the class interesting.

This item is likely to elicit full agreement from all participants, and is thus unlikely to tell the researcher much that is useful. It is therefore best to include items that discriminate between participants in the study. In other words, try to use items that will provoke as full a range of answers as possible.

Another problem inherent in Likert Scales is the fact that they may provoke a tendency among some participants to simply go down the scale circling the same number for every item. One way to ensure that they do not do this is to include both positively and negatively worded items. For example, if a participant agrees fully with the item:

I like learning grammar.

Then logically, they should disagree with the item:

I dislike learning grammar.

If they have put the same response for both of these items then it will immediately be clear that they have not been filling in the questionnaire properly. It is important to remember with reversed items that when the researcher is entering the data into a spreadsheet he or she should reverse the scores. So, for example, if the aim of the study is to measure the extent to which a group of learners enjoys learning grammar then a score of five in response to the sentence 'I dislike learning grammar' will need to be converted to a score of one.

A further problem inherent in Likert Scales is that of central tendency error. Sometimes participants like to hedge their bets and only use the middle points on the scale. There are two main ways of overcoming this problem. One is to have a scale from one to seven, but this can make it difficult to label every point on the scale. Another solution is to use a scale from one to five and to remind the participants verbally and in writing to use the whole scale wherever possible. Some researchers believe that you should always have an even number of items in a Likert scale in order to force the respondent to make a choice (i.e. there is no 'neutral' option). Others believe that a neutral option is useful or even essential; forcing a choice may involve forcing respondents to state an opinion that they do not actually hold.

To sum up, when using questionnaire research in applied linguistics, it is important to think carefully about a number of issues. Firstly, the researcher must make sure that he or she is able to pilot the questionnaire on a similar group of respondents to those who will be consulted in the main study. Then the researcher must consider whether it will be better to administer it in a face-to-face context, by post or e-mail, or via a specialist questionnaire hosting website such as SurveyMonkey (www. surveymonkey.com). It is important to remember that the questionnaire is only ever going to reveal what the respondents *think* they do, rather than what they actually do. The questions are the *researcher's* questions and were not put together by the participants themselves, and this may therefore shape the answers that are given.

Collecting other types of quantitative data

Of course, not all quantitative data collection will be through the use of questionnaires. Sometimes it will take the form of test results or involve counting the numbers of different types of utterances produced by students, or different types of activities employed by teachers. In text analysis it can consist of numbers of different types of utterances or gestures used in particular situations. A number of observation schedules exist that can be adapted to a wide variety of research settings. A good example of an observation schedule is Dörnyei's (2007) 'Motivation Orientation of Language Teaching' (MOLT). In this schedule, the researcher makes minute-by-minute tick-box recordings of the different ways in which the teacher generates and maintains motivation. These include: the ways in which the teacher makes effective use of discourse (such as signposting, establishing relevance, scaffolding and promoting cooperation); the use of activities that are likely to promote motivation (such as pair or group work and the use of activities that involve tangible rewards); ways of encouraging positive self-evaluation in the students (such as the elicitation of self- and peer-correction and the use of effective praise); and evidence of motivated behaviour by the students (such as the proportion of students who eagerly volunteer and participate). This schedule provides the researcher with quantitative data that can then be used to assess the level of motivation among their students in the classroom.

Another area of research that requires the collection of large quantities of data which are then analysed statistically is research into the relative merits of different teaching approaches. Earlier in this chapter, for example, we saw that Derwing *et al.* (2007) were interested in measuring the fluency and comprehensibility of their participants. They simply used two seven-point Likert Scales, one for fluency (where 1 = extremely fluent and 7 = extremely dysfluent) and one for comprehensibility (where 1 = very easy to understand and 7 = extremely difficult to understand) and asked 23 raters to rate the fluency and comprehensibility of the participants using these scales.

Other researchers have measured fluency, accuracy and complexity by focusing in detail on the linguistic features of the language produced (e.g. Bygate *et al.* 2009; Ellis and Barkhuizen 2005). Bygate *et al.* were interested in the effects of diffent types of task on the nature of the language produced by learners. In order to investigate this, they made detailed measurements of fluency, accuracy and complexity and then conducted statistical tests to identify whether or not there was a relationship between any of them and the tasks used. In this study, task type and learning conditions would be described as *independent* variables, whereas fluency, accuracy and complexity would be described as *dependent* variables (in other words they are thought to depend on, or be influenced by, the independent variables). Of the three dependent variables, accuracy can be measured fairly objectively by counting the number of mistakes made and taking this as a reverse indicator of accuracy. Fluency can also be measured fairly objectively by counting the number of pauses. Complexity would be fairly easy to measure in written output as one could focus on the number of subordinate and coordinate clauses used, but in spoken language production complexity poses more of a challenge. It might make sense here to break the concept down into different types of complexity.

Conclusion

In this chapter we have introduced several techniques that applied linguists use to collect quantitative data. We have seen that a sample can never be viewed as a perfect mirror of the target population that we are hoping to make claims about, but that there are certain measures that we can take to improve the generalisability of our findings. Although generalisability is important, it is not enough – it does not follow that generalisable quantitative findings are important or interesting findings. To establish whether findings are significant we need to perform statistical tests on our data.

8
Analysing quantitative data

Introduction

In Chapter 7 we looked at a number of ways in which applied linguists gather quantitative data. In this chapter we look at some of the tests that applied linguists use to analyse these data once they have obtained them. In other words, we will be turning our attention in this chapter to statistics. There are many ways of analysing quantitative data and your choice of statistical technique will depend on the kind of data you have collected and on the kinds of things you want to find out from them. Statistical analysis falls into two broad categories – descriptive and inferential – and applied linguists use both. In the applied linguistics literature, you will often come across references to various statistical tests. In this chapter, we discuss and exemplify some of the most commonly used statistical tests, using practical examples from a variety of applied linguistic studies. Our aim in this chapter is not to provide detailed information about specific statistical tests, but to show some examples of the sorts of questions that can be addressed through statistical studies and the types of things that statistics can and cannot tell us about our data. Applied linguistics students who come from arts and humanities backgrounds find the thought of doing statistics somewhat daunting at first. However, when you actually start using statistics, you will find that they are not that difficult to understand, and with the software packages that are now available, the analyses themselves are surprisingly easy to do.

The key skill, as we will see later in this chapter, lies in being able to choose a statistical test that is appropriate to the question you are interested in, and the data you have collected about it.

Descriptive and inferential statistics

Quantitative researchers make a basic distinction between two kinds of statistics: *descriptive* statistics and *inferential* statistics. As the name suggests, descriptive statistics provide us with basic numerical information about the phenomenon we are interested in studying. Inferential statistics, in contrast, tell us how meaningful this information is. Inferential statistics also give an indication of how generalisable our findings are, and tell us whether, if we were to conduct the study again in a similar setting, we would be likely to come up with a similar set of results. Let us illustrate this with an example from the applied linguistics literature. Vidal (2003) was interested in discovering whether or not listening to lectures in English improved the vocabulary range of second language learners. Her exact research question was as follows:

> *What is the effect of listening to academic lectures on EFL vocabulary acquisition (as measured by pre- and post-test scores)?*

In order to answer this research question, she collected data from a group of students studying Tourism and English for Specific Purposes at a university in Madrid, Spain. She began by conducting a pre-test, in which she measured their knowledge of a number of English words by asking them to provide a translation of each word and to use it in an English sentence. The responses were scored 1–5 and the average, or *mean*, score for each student was calculated. She then had them watch three video-recorded lectures on the economic, socio-cultural and environmental impacts of tourism. These lectures contained the words that had been used in the pre-test. A month after they had attended the lectures, she tested them again, in a post-test, on their knowledge of the words. The mean scores on the pre- and post-tests are shown in Table 8.1.

Table 8.1 Mean scores on the pre- and post-tests in Vidal's study.

Test	Mean score	Number of students	Standard deviation
Pre-test	1.4	116	3.5
Post-test	16.38	116	17.56

These scores appear to indicate that the students in Vidal's study had made a huge improvement in their knowledge of these words. Their mean scores leapt from 1.4 to 16.38. However, we must not jump to conclusions as these are only descriptive statistical data and we do not yet have any statistical 'proof' that this difference is significant. Certainly, the difference between the two means in Table 8.1 is impressive, and it is also true that the number of participants in the study was quite large (116). But let us look more closely at the third column in the table. This shows something called the standard deviation. This should be reported (along with the sample size or 'N') whenever a mean score is given. The standard deviation tells us about the spread of the scores across the students. On the pre-test the standard deviation is quite small, which means that they all received a score that was fairly close to the mean. On the post-test however, the standard deviation (or 'spread') is very large, which means that while some students did extremely well on the test, others did very badly. Therefore attending lectures appeared to help some students a great deal with their vocabulary acquisition, but not all of them benefitted. This large standard deviation may therefore detract somewhat from the overall significance of the finding. On the other hand it does raise some interesting additional questions (such as why was there so much variation?), which could fruitfully be explored through qualitative analysis.

Vidal (2003) tells us that the difference between the means was in fact significant ($p<0.01$). What this means is that the probability (p) of her having found that result completely by accident is less than one in a hundred (i.e. 0.01). Therefore, if she conducted exactly the same experiment again, 100 times (not that one would ever do this!) one would expect to achieve the same result 99 times. Across the social sciences, 0.01 and 0.05 are the two cut-off points that statisticians have agreed to use as indicators of significance. If $p<0.01$, the results tend to be reported as being 'highly significant'. Whereas if $p<0.05$, they tend to be reported as being simply 'significant'. The 'p' value is calculated using the mean scores of the samples, the sample sizes, and the standard deviation of the samples (i.e. all the information that is in Table 8.1). Generally speaking, the larger the sample sizes, the greater the difference between the mean scores, and the smaller the standard deviations, the smaller p is likely to be and the more significant the result is.

In the following section, we provide an example showing how a researcher might use a statistics package to calculate the p value in a case such as this. If you are interested in doing such a study yourself, we recommend one of the excellent guides in the area, such as Larson-Hall (2009) or Pallant (2005). These guides contain clear, practical and very detailed accounts of how to perform a range of statistical tests. Vidal's study involved a far more complex set of variables than those we have discussed here, and as we have seen above, it involved large numbers of participants. It would therefore be impossible for us to replicate what she did here. So instead, let us take an imaginary set of data from a much smaller number of student participants (five) and use this to demonstrate a very simple statistical technique that can be used to calculate whether or not our students have made a significant improvement on a particular test. The test we outline is somewhat simpler than the one used in Vidal's study, but its use would be valid in such a study.

Modern statistics packages have made it very easy to carry out inferential statistics. One of the most widely-used statistics packages in applied linguistics is the 'Statistics Package for Social Scientists' or 'SPSS'. Although this is not the only statistics package available on the market, it is widely used in educational settings and is often available on campus networks and can be purchased cheaply by students. There are also a number of powerful freeware packages, such as 'R' (www.r-project.org) but the problem with these is that the interface can be off-putting for people who have no previous experience with statistics, or who are not comfortable with command-line interfaces. An excellent, straightforward book on how to use SPSS is Pallant (2005). If you would like to learn how to do these tests in SPSS, we recommend that you follow the instructions in Pallant's book. We will refer to SPSS in the example below.

Establishing whether or not an improvement in students' vocabulary knowledge is statistically significant

Let us begin by looking again at Vidal's research question:

What is the effect of listening to academic lectures on EFL vocabulary acquisition (as measured by pre- and post-test scores)?

If we were to analyse our findings statistically in order to answer this question, we would probably begin by entering the pre- and post-test scores into a spreadsheet. Although it is possible to enter the scores directly into a statistics package, it is better to use an Excel (or similar) spreadsheet as these are easier to manipulate and can easily be opened within different statistics packages. It is important to enter the data in a completely raw form and not to do anything with them before putting them into your spreadsheet. For the sake of simplicity, let us imagine that we have done the study with just five participants, and that the tests are scored out of ten (in reality we would never use such a small number of participants in a statistical study such as this). The spreadsheet might look something like this:

Table 8.2 Imaginary scores on the pre- and post-tests.

Participant	Pre-test scores	Post-test scores
1	2	6
2	6	8
3	3	7
4	4	10
5	2	9
Mean score	3.4	8

Looking at these scores, it certainly seems that there was some improvement in the students' speaking ability. The mean score on the pre-test is 3.4 and the mean score on the post-test is 8. There has therefore been an average improvement of 4.6. We now need to find out whether this difference is statistically significant.

Having placed the data into a spreadsheet file, the first thing to do is to save and close the file. We would then need to open the file in a statistics package. When we have opened the data in SPSS we need to make an important decision. There are two types of statistical tests that we can use here, depending on the nature of the data. If we have a large, normally distributed sample with data that are continuously distributed we can use a powerful form of statistics called parametric statistics. These are the best statistics to use if at all possible as they are robust and reliable. However, we may have a small sample which is not normally distributed. In this case we need to use a different type of statistics called nonparametric statistics. If we use nonparametric statistics we need to be more tentative about the sorts of claims we make regarding the results.

But what exactly do the words 'large' and 'normally distributed' mean? Statisticians sometimes use the word 'large' to refer to a sample of over 30 participants. However, if we are conducting a study looking at relationships between several subgroups within a sample we would need more than this. As a basic rule, the smallest subgroup must contain 30 participants in order to allow the use of parametric statistics. With numbers lower than this, we should consider using nonparametric statistics.

What exactly does 'normally distributed' mean? If we take just about any human trait and we measure it in a large enough group of people, we will nearly always find that there is a small number of people at the extremes of the scale with very low or very high levels of that trait, and that the majority of the population will fall somewhere in the middle. The distribution of levels of this trait across a large group of people will pretty much always look something like Figure 8.1. This is called the *normal distribution*. We can see from this diagram that the majority of participants receive scores that are somewhere in the middle of the range and that the curve is completely symmetrical. If we have this sort of distribution (which is easy enough to find out as most statistical packages have an option that allows you to see the spread of your data represented graphically), then we can use the more powerful 'parametric' statistics.

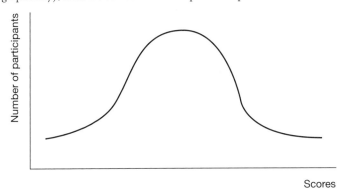

Figure 8.1 **The normal distribution curve.**

The data in Table 8.2 above are clearly from a very small sample and are thus highly unlikely to be normally distributed. We would therefore need to treat the data as non-parametric data, and we would need to use something called a Wilcoxon signed ranks test. Despite its intimidating-sounding name, this is a very straightforward test to do in SPSS and a very clear account of how to do it can be found in Pallant (2005). The SPSS output tells us what the p value is, and we need to look at this to see whether it is less than 0.05. If so, this would give us a significant result, allowing us to say that:

By means of a Wilcoxon signed ranks test I was able to establish that there was a significant improvement in the test scores of the participants ($p<0.05$).

What this means is that the probability (p) of us having found that result completely by accident is less than five in a hundred (i.e. 0.05). Therefore, if we conducted exactly the same experiment again 100 times, we would expect to achieve the same result 95 times.

If the data had been from a large, normally distributed sample, we would have used a test called a paired samples t-test as the students are all from the same group. (As with all of the statistical tests discussed in this chapter, paired samples t-tests are accessed via the 'analyse' menu in SPSS.) It could be that the students' vocabulary test scores would have improved anyway, whether or not they had attended the lectures. In Vidal's study this is unlikely as the vocabulary items were closely tied to the lecture content. In other studies, however, the learning that is being measured is not as closely tied to the content of what is being taught. In these cases it is necessary to compare the improvement made by the participants in our study with that of a group of students who have not received any special training. In statistical parlance, these two groups are usually referred to as the 'experimental group' and the 'control group' respectively. In the next section we look at an applied linguistic study that involved an experimental group and a control group.

Do students who have been taught through a task-based learning approach exhibit better L2 oral production than those who have been taught through a more traditional communicative approach?

Our next example focuses on a study by De Ridder *et al.* (2007). The authors of this study hypothesised that students who had been taught through a task-based learning approach (see Chapters 2, 3 and 9 for further details of this approach) would exhibit higher levels of L2 production than students who had been taught via a more traditional communicative approach. The reason why they made this hypothesis is that they believe the task-based learning approach provides more opportunities for vocabulary recycling and that it encourages learners to be more creative with the language they had already learned. In order to test this hypothesis, they took 68 Dutch-speaking students of Spanish for Business and Economics at a Belgian university (35 in the control group and 33 in the experimental group). The students in the experimental group received task-based instruction and the students in the control group received traditional communicative language teaching. They then gave the students in the two groups oral examinations and the performance of the students was scored by two independent evaluators for: pronunciation, fluency, intonation, sociolinguistic competence, lexis and grammar. Their results were presented as follows (p. 312):

(a)   The control group outperformed the experimental group on pronunciation [t (66) = -3.53, p (two tailed) = 0.001] and intonation [t (66) = -2.73, p (two tailed) = 0.008]. This contradicts the hypothesis.

(b)   The experimental group outperformed the control group on grammar [t (66)¼6.06, p (two tailed) = 0.000], vocabulary [t (66) = 5.51, p (two tailed) = 0.000], and sociolinguistic competence [t (66) = 5.52, p (two tailed) = 0.000]. This supports the hypothesis.

(c)   No significant difference could be established on fluency. This also contradicts the hypothesis.

What these results mean are that the students in the control group performed significantly better than the students in the experimental group on intonation and pronunciation accuracy, whereas the students in the experimental group performed significantly better than the control group on grammar, vocabulary and sociolinguistic competence. There were no significant differences in terms of fluency and all of these results were based on an independent samples t-test. But what is an independent samples t-test and what does it measure?

In order to illustrate this, let us look at some more simplified data. If De Ridder *et al.* had only had five students in each group, they would have entered their data into a spreadsheet in the manner shown in Table 8.3. Again, we are only using five students to illustrate the procedure. In order to be reliable, this sort of test would normally require at least 30 participants.

Table 8.3 **Grammar scores received by the students in each group.**

Participant	Group	Grammar score
1	1	8
2	1	6
3	1	9
4	1	4
5	1	8
6	2	2
7	2	5
8	2	4
9	2	3
10	2	5

Notice here that we have entered all the participants into a single column and that we have added a column saying which group they are in. '1' means that they are in the experimental group and '2' means that they are in the control group. If we calculated the mean scores for participants in the experimental group and participants in the control group we would see that the grammar scores skills of the students in the experimental group is much higher than that of the students in the control group.

In order to calculate whether this difference is significant, we would use a Mann-Whitney U test. If the data had been from a large, normally distributed sample, we would have used an independent samples t-test as the students are from different groups. Again, these tests are described in Pallant (2005) and again we would look for the p value in the output. If this was less than 0.05 we would be able to say that our findings were significant.

So far we have just looked at two types of statistical analysis that are often used in the applied linguistics literature. We have seen how a researcher might use statistics to assess whether their students have improved significantly in a certain area of language competence, and we have seen how a research might use statistical analysis to compare the benefits of one teaching technique with those of another technique. We now turn to two further, somewhat more sophisticated techniques. The first technique, correlation analysis, allows us to determine whether different learner traits or skills (such as writing and speaking performance) are related to one another. The second technique, factor analysis, tells us whether certain preferences for types of activities or approaches to learning group together in the learners' minds.

Is L2 writing performance related to speaking performance?

Yu (2009) was interested in exploring the extent to which L2 writing performance was related to speaking performance. He was particularly interested in the concept of lexical diversity, which refers to the range of vocabulary items that the student produces in a particular piece of work. He hypothesized that if a student was able to use a wide range of vocabulary when writing in the target language he or she would also be able to use a wide range of vocabulary when speaking it. In other words, Yu predicted that there would be a correlation between the two variables. In order to test this hypothesis, he calculated the type/token ratios (i.e. the number of *different* words as a proportion of the number of *total* words in a text) in written and spoken test data produced by 201 candidates who had taken the Test of English as a Foreign Language (TOEFL), which is an English language test that non-English-speaking international students need to pass in order to gain access to US universities. He then compared the type-token ratios in the written data with those in the spoken data. He found a statistically significant correlation between the two scores ($p < 0.05$).

In order to see what this means and to understand how Yu carried out his analysis, let us look at some simplified data. In order to assess whether or not there was a significant correlation between the two sets of lexical diversity scores, the researcher would probably begin by entering the scores into a spreadsheet as seen in Table 8.4.

Table 8.4 **Lexical diversity in writing and speaking.**

Participant	Lexical diversity in writing	Lexical diversity in speaking
1	2	1
2	5	4
3	10	6
4	9	8
5	3	2

In order to calculate whether lexical diversity in writing correlates with lexical diversity in speaking, we would use a test called a Spearman's rho correlation. If the data had been from a large, normally distributed sample, we would have used a Pearson's correlation test, which is also available in SPSS. As with the other tests, a detailed description of how to perform these very straightforward tests using SPSS can be found in Pallant (2005). If we entered these particular data into such a test, we would get a significant correlation of $p<0.05$, which means that there is a significant relationship between the two variables. In other words, if students display lexical diversity in their writing, they will also show it in their speaking.

Can aspects of student behaviour or learning preferences be classified into meaningful groups?

The final statistical test that we will look at in this chapter is factor analysis. This procedure allows the researcher to identify relationships between a large number of variables and to explain these relationships in terms of their common underlying features (or factors). The technique is becoming increasingly popular among applied linguists who are interested in exploring how the different variables in their data group together. It is particularly widely used in corpus linguistics (see Chapter 10), and in language learning strategy research, where it is becoming unacceptable to propose categories of strategies that are based on the researcher's intuition alone. Through factor analysis, it is possible to see how the various strategies that are available to language learners are grouped together in the learners' minds. For example, Hsiao and Oxford

(2002) administered a language learning strategy questionnaire to 517 students of English from a range of different backgrounds. Through a factor analysis they found that some of the strategies represented in the questionnaire grouped together naturally in the learners' minds. Their findings challenged some of the traditional views in the relevant literature. For instance, they discovered that rather than viewing 'cognitive' strategies as a unitary phenomenon (which is how they had previously been presented in some of the literature), the participants in their study subconsciously grouped them into 'memory-based', 'cognitive' and 'compensatory' strategies. The crucial point to note here is that these groups of strategies were identified - and could only have been identified - using a computer-assisted factor analysis. It would have been impossible for Hsiao and Oxford to have discovered these groupings manually, given the very large and complex nature of the data set that they were working with.

Hsiao and Oxford's methodology is too lengthy to reproduce in full here, but to illustrate the procedure, we will use a simplified example. In this example, a teacher of young learners is interested in investigating the types of activities that her learners find motivating. In order to do so, she asks her learners to rate on a scale from 1–5, how motivating they find the following activities:

1   Acting out plays
2   Talking to classmates
3   Singing pop songs
4   Writing poems
5   Drawing pictures
6   Discussing ideas with classmates
7   Listening to the radio
8   Working in pairs
9   Reading magazines
10 Doing project work in groups

Say, for example, the study was conducted with five participants (in reality we would of course need far more than this), they might provide the answers as seen in Table 8.5.

Table 8.5 **Answers given on a Likert Scale by young learners who were asked how motivating they found ten activities.**

Participant	Item 1	Item 2	Item 3	Item 4	Item 5	Item 6	Item 7	Item 8	Item 9	Item 10
1	1	2	3	3	3	2	2	1	2	3
2	2	3	5	5	3	5	4	3	4	5
3	5	5	5	4	3	1	5	2	5	2
4	4	4	1	4	4	3	2	4	1	1
5	2	5	2	1	2	4	1	5	2	4

Notice that participant 5 has given similarly high responses to items (i.e. activities) 2, 6, 8 and 10. This could be because they have somehow perceived these activities as being somehow similar to one another. If we look back at the activities themselves we can see that each of them involves communication with classmates. If more than one participant perceived them as being similar to one another than we might find that they would answer in the same way for all three activities, which would make these items into some sort of group or 'factor'. We might decide to label the factor as 'learning through peer interaction'.

Factor analysis is useful because it enables the researcher to identify relationships between items that the participants themselves may have perceived, but which the researcher may not have thought of. It thus provides an *objective* manner of identifying the way in which certain items group together. In order to find out if any of the items in the above study grouped together, we would need to use SPSS to carry out a factor analysis test. Again, Pallant (2005) provides an excellent step-by-step explanation of how to do this. If we did this test with the above data, the computer would display a results table that looks something like that in Table 8.6.

Table 8.6 **A possible results table from a factor analysis.**

	Factor 1	Factor 2	Factor 3	Factor 4
Item 1	0.225	**0.763**	-0.419	**0.437**
Item 2	0.087	**0.963**	-0.072	-0.246
Item 3	**0.985**	-0.165	0.030	0.042
Item 4	**0.459**	-0.156	0.060	**0.873**
Item 5	-0.240	-0.040	-0.249	**0.938**
Item 6	-0.126	-0.043	**0.991**	-0.010
Item 7	**0.990**	0.128	-0.062	0.012
Item 8	-0.437	**0.669**	**0.577**	-0.162
Item 9	**0.990**	0.128	-0.062	0.012
Item 10	0.388	-0.343	**0.737**	-0.435

The four components that appear across the top refer to the four 'groups' or 'factors' of items that have emerged from the analysis. In other words, they refer to the four factors into which the items appear to have fallen. Of course the computer program is not clever enough to know what exactly these groups are so it has given them the labels 1, 2, 3 and 4. Labelling the factors in a more meaningful way is the researcher's job. To do this, one needs to see which items 'load on' the factors most strongly, and then work out what it is that these items have in common. Items which are said to load on particular factors are those that have a value of more than 0.4 in Table 8.6. These have been highlighted in bold.

Factor 1
Singing pop songs (item 3)
Writing poems (item 4)
Listening to the radio (item 7)
Reading magazines (item 9)

This factor might thus be labelled something like 'learning by doing'.

Factor 2
Acting out plays (item 1)
Talking to classmates (item 2)
Working in pairs (item 8)

This factor could be labelled something like 'learning through oral communication'.

Factor 3
Discussing ideas with classmates (item 6)
Working in pairs (item 8)
Doing project work in groups (item 10)

This factor could be labelled something like 'learning through communication with peers'.

Factor 4
Acting out plays (item 1)
Writing poems (item 4)
Drawing pictures (item 5)

This factor could be labelled something like 'learning through artistic/ creative activities'.

By grouping the items into factors in this way, researchers can gain insights into the sorts of activities that could be said to cluster together in the minds of their participants, and study these groups of activities rather than looking at each activity individually. This provides a more robust approach to the study of behaviour and prevents the researcher from imposing his or her own categories on the data.

Bringing it all together: the role of language aptitude in first language attrition

A good example of a study that involves a combination of several of the qualitative research methods discussed above is Bylund et al.'s (2009) study of the relationship between language aptitude and first language attrition. Some applied linguists have been interested in exploring why it is that some people simply appear to be better at learning languages than others and possess what is sometimes referred to as 'a flair for languages'. They are keen to find out whether such a thing as a talent for language learning exists, independent of general intelligence. They have suggested that some people possess some sort of aptitude for language learning and that this aptitude consists of a number of discrete characteristics that predispose certain people to be particularly good at learning languages. These characteristics are measured by a 'Modern Language Aptitude Test'.[1]

First language attrition refers to the fact that when people go to live in another country and learn a new language, they tend to forget elements of their first language (or 'mother tongue'). Bylund *et al.* hypothesised that people with higher levels of language aptitude are less likely to suffer from language attrition when they move abroad as their general language learning/analysis skills will compensate for the lack of exposure they are receiving with respect to their first language. In order to test their hypothesis they took a group of individuals who had left their home country (Spain) and who had been living abroad in Sweden since their early teens. They measured their language aptitude of all the participants using the Modern Language Aptitude Test and gave them a Spanish grammar test. They began by carrying out an independent samples t-test to compare the results of the Spanish grammar test with those of a group of Spanish-speakers who had not left their Spanish-speaking homeland. They found that there was a significant difference ($p < 0.05$) between the scores received by the participants who had not left their homeland and those who had. As one would expect, the partcipants who had stayed at home scored better.

Bylund *et al.* then carried out a Pearson correlation test on those participants who had left their homeland and found a significant correlation between language aptitude and scores on the Spanish grammar test ($p < 0.05$). These findings allowed them to conclude that language aptitude can compensate for the linguistic attrition effects of time spent away from one's own country.

Throughout their study, Bylund *et al.* talk about various 'factors' that contribute to this effect. These include the degree of contact with the first language, the level of proficiency in the new language, the age of the participants, their age when they moved countries, their reasons for moving country and so on. A next step in their study might therefore be to conduct a factor analysis to see if any of these factors cluster together in meaningful ways. Another useful follow-up would be to conduct in-depth interviews with those participants in the study who displayed exceptionally high or low levels of grammatical ability in Spanish, and to further explore the affective factors that may have influenced their performance. Here we are getting into the realms of mixed-methods research, an area to which we now turn.

Mixed-methods research

In many studies, the researchers involved feel that neither quantitative nor qualitative research methods can provide the full picture they need in order to answer their research questions. The usual problem is that quantitative approaches will provide a broad yet somewhat superficial set of answers, whereas qualitative approaches will provide in-depth answers that may not be readily applicable to a wide range of participants. In such cases, an ideal solution may be to combine them in order to create a *mixed methods* approach. The researcher may begin with a large quantitative survey, and then pick out a number of interesting cases for more in-depth qualitative analysis, or they may start with a qualitative analysis with a small focus group and use this to identify features that would be worthy of quantitative investigation with a larger sample.

Some research techniques blur the boundaries between qualitative and quantitative and can involve both approaches at once. An example of one such technique is that employed by Poupore (2008 and forthcoming). Poupore was interested in establishing whether different types of tasks provoked different levels of motivation in Korean university-level students of English. As well as looking for overall statistically significant differences between the tasks, he was interested in exploring the complexity of the situation in more depth. One thing that he was particularly interested in was how levels of motivation changed over the duration of the task. He therefore conducted a study in which he asked the participants to stop at five-minute intervals and to record on a chart how motivated they felt by the task at that point. He averaged out their responses and came up with a graph representing eight of his tasks (see Figure 8.2).

In order to account for some of the ups and downs in this graph, he carried out a detailed qualitative investigation of the individual characteristics of the tasks, and the ways in which the students had handled them as a group. As well as focusing on the tasks themselves, his investigation took account of a number of variables which cannot easily be measured in quantitative terms. These included group work dynamic (social dynamic existing within the groups) and learner-based traits such as overall L2 motivation and L2 anxiety. By carrying out a qualitative study of these variables (through interviews and the collection of verbal and non-verbal data through observation and transcription), he was able to paint a detailed picture of what was going on 'behind the graph'.

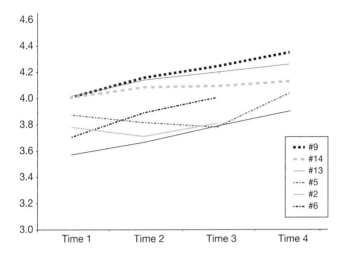

Figure 8.2 **Graph showing different levels of motivation at different points during the different tasks by students in Poupore's (2008) study.**

As you may have noticed, many of the examples that we have used in this and the previous three chapters have been taken from PhD research projects. This being the case, you may at this point be wondering what the difference is between an MA dissertation and a PhD thesis (or 'an MA thesis and a PhD dissertation' in some countries). The main difference is one of scope. Master's-level dissertations tend to focus on fewer variables than PhD theses. They also tend to involve fewer participants and fewer activities. At MA level, it is not usually necessary to have a large normally-distributed random sample of participants. The aim of an MA dissertation is to explore one's hypotheses and/or to refine one's research methodologies, rather than to produce definitive, influential research findings that can be published in an academic journal (although some outstanding MA-level work does manage to do this). An MA dissertation should set out to make an original contribution to the field but this contribution will necessarily be more modest than that of a PhD thesis. An MA student might, for example, aim to test the effectiveness of a particular approach to teaching in their own country on their own particular students, or they may investigate the role of gender differences

125

in the context of an already-established theory, or they may choose to study the classroom interaction patterns in their own teaching settings to establish the extent to which existing models of interaction apply to that particular setting. The findings of most MA dissertations will generally be more locally-relevant than those of a PhD thesis.

Conclusion

In this and the previous chapter we have provided a brief overview of some of the reasons why applied linguists collect and analyse quantitative data, and the ways in which they do it. We have seen that the general aim is to study a sample of participants and to employ data collection techniques that make the data as generalisable as possible. Statistical techniques are then employed to *objectively* assess which findings are significant and therefore worthy of reporting. One of the weaknesses of quantitative research is that it tends to provide a rather 'broad brush' approach. It may tell us, for example, that, on the whole, male students tend to employ different language learning strategies from female students, but it will never be able to tell us why this is so, or how the students go about selecting their strategies according to the demand of the task. Nor will it tell us much about the unpredictable, complex, non-linear aspects of human behaviour that so often demand attention in applied linguistics research data. For this we need to turn back to the qualitative approaches reviewed earlier in this book.

9

Analysing texts

Introduction

Much applied linguistic research focuses on texts. This chapter begins by explaining what texts are, and how the concept of 'text' relates to the equally important concept of 'discourse' in applied linguistics. We then consider why texts and discourses are of such interest and importance in applied linguistics, before looking in detail at two contrasting examples of text analysis research in action.

What is a text?

We will answer this question by making five basic observations about texts, as follows:

1 Texts are the products of human communication

Texts may consist entirely of written or spoken language; they may consist exclusively of visual images; or they may contain a combination of visual and verbal modes. Texts may also include sound (often in websites), texture, perhaps even smell (e.g. scented love letters). Texts that combine 'semiotic modes' are known as 'multimodal' texts; texts that consist of one mode only are thus sometimes called 'monomodal' texts. Arguably, however, all texts are multimodal, as each will be written on a certain type of paper (thus including a tactile dimension that may in itself be meaningful to some degree – think of high-quality office paper, for example) or use certain fonts and a particular style of layout (thus including a clear visual dimension). In any case, texts can take many and various forms. Casual conversations, books, newspaper articles, academic lectures, political speeches, television news reports, plays, road signs, websites and Neolithic cave paintings are all forms of text.

2 Texts are complete functional units

A play or a newspaper article is a text, but a line of dialogue from a play or an extract from a newspaper article is not – such data are usually referred to as *extracts*, *samples* or *examples*. This does not mean that texts are defined according to their length, however. On the contrary, a single sound, image or orthographic character can be a complete text, as long as it is performing a clear function in its own right. A famous example of this is the telegram that the nineteenth-century French writer Victor Hugo wrote to his publisher, when he wanted to find out how well his novel *Les Miserables* was selling. Hugo simply wrote '?', and received the equally economical reply '!'.

3 Texts can be constructed by one person, or 'co-constructed' by two or more people

Written texts are frequently composed by single individuals, although this is clearly not always the case, as the book you are currently holding in your hands attests! Conversely, many if not most spoken texts are the product of communicative interaction among two or more people; the classic case here is casual conversation. But again, this is not always so; speeches given at public events, for example, are usually made by single individual speakers.

4 Texts always have at least one addressee

That is, every text is produced for someone. Usually, texts are produced with another person in mind (for example in a text message to a friend, a telephone conversation with a call centre employee or an essay for a teacher), but they can also be produced for one's own self (for example, in a diary entry, a reminder note or a shopping list). Perhaps it might be more accurate to say 'almost always', because there probably are cases where the producer of a text has no one in particular in mind (e.g. a drawing produced by a very small child, or a doodle drawn on a photocopied handout by a bored adult at a business meeting). But even here one could argue that such texts are still being produced for the benefit of the text-producers themselves.

5 Texts always have at least one purpose

In a very general sense, nearly all texts have the same purpose – to communicate. More specifically, nearly all texts have at least one more particular communicative motivation. We produce texts in order to inform, to persuade, to entertain, to warn and to entreat, among many other things, and it is these more specific purposes that applied linguists are particularly interested in. It is of course often the case that a text will aim to do several of these things at the same time. Even apparently trivial texts such as casual conversations about the weather are still deeply purposeful, in that they serve to create or maintain social bonds between individuals. So too are even those texts that are not clearly motivated by communicative needs. The drawing produced by the small child may be an expression of that child's feelings, or an opportunity to practise holding and controlling a pen, while the doodle drawn by the bored office worker may perform the valuable function of relieving tedium or venting feelings of frustration. Of course, the purpose of the text may not be shared by addresser and addressee – this is often called 'talking at cross purposes'. There are also instances where the real purpose of the text is kept hidden from the audience, as we will see later.

Text analysis and discourse analysis

In applied linguistics, texts are generally not seen as interesting in themselves, but as interesting for what they reveal about the 'discourses' that have produced them. It is for this reason that the relevant subfield of applied linguistics that focuses on texts is called 'discourse analysis' and not 'text analysis'.

'Discourse' is one of the most popular – but also one of the most controversial and contested – concepts in applied linguistics (and in the humanities and social sciences more generally), and the activity of discourse analysis is practised in a correspondingly wide variety of ways. For our purposes, however, it is possible to identify two main uses or understandings of the term 'discourse' in applied linguistics today. The first of these defines discourse as the process of linguistic interaction, of which texts are the end products or residual traces. The participants in a conversation construct a discourse, and the text is the product of that interaction. In writing it is somewhat different – when we read a text we construct a discourse from it, by trying to enter into an imaginary dialogue with the author. Conversely, when we write a text we imagine how the reader will react to each thing that we tell them, and we try to guide their interpretation of the text so that they retrieve our intended meaning from it. In short, the concept of discourse as interaction is interested in how people make meanings from texts. This includes considerations both of the ways in which speakers and writers attempt to influence listeners and readers, and the ways in which listeners and readers pick up on (or do not pick up on) such rhetorical cues.

The other broad approach to discourse in applied linguistics sees discourses as sets of conventionalised meanings and values that are associated with particular social groups. From this perspective, the goal of discourse analysis is to investigate how these value systems are produced, reproduced, challenged and appropriated in and through texts. For example, we might look at how and to what extent conversations among and between men and women reproduce or challenge certain gender stereotypes. Alternatively, we might be interested in studying whether particular news media sources present a war as inevitable or avoidable, or as desirable or undesirable. How is discourse a 'process' in this sense? It is a process in the sense that each individual text makes a small but significant contribution to the ongoing process of values construction – in the same way that each day's weather contributes to the overall climate in a particular geographical location.

Practicalities of data collection and storage

Before moving on to look in detail at some of the ways in which applied linguists go about analysing interaction patterns and value systems in texts, we want to offer some practical advice on the more mundane (but equally important) issue of how texts and text-analytical data should be collected and stored. As much of this advice essentially reiterates points already made in the preceding four chapters (where we discussed qualitative and quantitative research methods in detail), we will be brief here.

First of all, once you have decided which text or texts you want to collect and use for study purposes, it is essential that you try wherever possible to obtain the permission of the person, business or institution to whom each text belongs. In the case of private data such as emails, casual conversations or student essays this is a matter of research ethics; and in the case of public data such as books, articles and webpages it is a matter of respecting international copyright laws.

If you are planning to study spoken texts, remember that such data are extremely time consuming to transcribe. It is also advisable to check that the recordings you plan to transcribe are actually of usable quality before you begin. If you are planning to record the data yourself you may find that this can be technically very difficult to achieve in practice, particularly if you are attempting to record interactions among larger groups of people. Hand-held recording devices are usually fine for recording individuals and small groups, but they will struggle to capture what each individual speaker is saying in a student-centred EFL classroom or around a large dining table at a busy restaurant.

In either case it is always a good idea to keep master copies of all your texts and store them in a separate place. This will protect your original electronic data from computer viruses and hardware crashes, and your original hard copies from coffee stains and children's scrawls.

Qualitative text analysis can easily be done using simple note-making procedures, but sophisticated software is now starting to appear for some forms of analysis. For example, if you are using the analytical frameworks and categories offered by systemic-functional linguistics then there are now software tools that partly automate the labelling process for you. However, if you do plan to use such tools you may well need to factor a certain amount of additional time into your research schedule while you are learning how to use this software.

Finally, if you want to perform a quantitative analysis on your text(s) you will need to decide whether some form of inferential statistical treatment is required (and if so, which tests are and are not appropriate), or whether descriptive statistics are adequate for your own particular research purposes. In either case it will be a good idea to store your results electronically in the form of a spreadsheet document. As well as providing a convenient way of storing and retrieving your data, modern spreadsheet software packages can do a lot of the basic mathematical and statistical work for you, and they can also generate graphs and charts that you can copy and paste into a coursework assignment or research paper. Storing data in spreadsheet form also means that it can be manipulated using specialist statistical analysis software packages such as SPSS or R.

Text analysis in action: two examples

Approaches to text and discourse analysis are many and varied; so much so, in fact, that it will not be possible for us to provide you with a comprehensive survey here. What we propose to do instead is give you a flavour of what text analysis involves, and of what insights it can yield, by presenting two example studies below. The first of these case study examples focuses on texts as records of interaction, and draws principally on the methodology of conversation analysis introduced in Chapter 6. The second uses the framework of systemic-functional linguistics, introduced very briefly in Chapter 2, and focuses on texts as instantiations of particular value systems.

Before moving on, we should note that not all approaches to text and discourse analysis involve one or the other of these forms of analysis. Indeed, quite a lot of text analysis in applied linguistics does not involve any kind of linguistic analysis at all. Applied linguists interested in language policy, for example, might only be interested in the substantive content of government policy documents, and have no need to submit such texts to any kind of formal or structural analysis. Similarly, 'critical' applied linguists prefer to interpret texts by applying various strands of critical theory (post-structuralism, postmodernism, post-colonialism, feminism, queer theory), and make little or no use of concepts and frameworks drawn from linguistics as it is currently defined. Our reasons for choosing to focus on the forms of text analysis that we have done are twofold: first, they are among the best-known and most widely used approaches in contemporary applied linguistics; and second, they are approaches that lend themselves to – indeed, require – detailed analysis and explication.

An example of interaction analysis

For our case study example of interaction analysis we have chosen a now classic piece of research by the British applied linguist Paul Seedhouse (1999). The aim of Seedhouse's project was to study different types of L2 classroom interaction, with a view towards identifying the particular pedagogic strengths and weaknesses of each. His analysis was based on a conversation analysis of a collection of 330 lesson transcripts from 14 countries. Interestingly, one type of interaction that Seedhouse found to be particularly problematic in his analysis was task-based interaction (TBI), which was (and remains) one of the most fashionable methodologies in ELT. Task-based interaction refers to interactions where students are focused on the completion of pedagogic tasks, 'task' being defined here as 'an activity which involves the use of language but in which the focus is on the outcome of the activity rather than on the language used to achieve that outcome' (Willis 1990: 127).

Seedhouse identifies two potential problems with TBI as a form of L2 pedagogy:

1. Tasks lead students to use a very narrow and restricted turn-taking system.
2. Tasks lead students to use language in a very minimal way.

To illustrate the first of these claims, let us look in detail at Box 9.1. In this extract, two learners (LI and L2) are engaged in what is commonly known as an 'information gap' task. Each student has a map containing half of the information required to complete the picture, and each must ask the other to share this information by using language only – the students cannot see each other's maps.

Box 9.1: **Extract 1 from Seedhouse (1999).**

---

1 **LI:** The road from the town to the Kampong Kelantan ... the coconut =
2 **L2:** = Again, again.
3 **LI:** The road is from the town to Kampong Kelantan (7.5 sec) the town is in the
4 Jason Bay.
5 **L2:** Again. The town, where is the town?
6 **LI:** The town is on the Jason Bay.
7 **L2::** The, road?
8 **LI:** The road is from the town to Kampong Kelantan (11.0 sec) OK?
9 **L2:** OK.
10 **LI:** The mountain is behind the beach and the Jason Bay (8.1 sec) The river is
   from
11 the jungle to the Desaru (9.7 sec) The mou- the volcano is above the Kampong
12 Kelantan (7.2 sec) The coconut tree is along the beach.

Below we reproduce Seedhouse's analysis of this extract in full, in order to give you some sense of what an in-depth conversation analysis of a spoken transcript looks like.

In line 1, LI provides one item of information to L2, then without checking whether L2 has noted the first piece of information (the two learners cannot see each other), proceeds with the second item of information. Because L2 has not finished noting the first piece of information, L2 makes (in line 2) a repetition request, which requires LI to backtrack. In line 7, L2 asks where the road is. In line 8, LI supplies the information, waits for 11.0 seconds, then makes a confirmation check ('OK?') to ascertain whether L2 has completed that subsection of the task. LI appears to be orienting his utterances to L2's difficulty in completing the task, since LI uses an identical sentence structure each time, and leaves pauses between different items of information. We can see these pauses in lines 3, 10, 11 and 12, and they vary from 7.2 seconds to 9.7 seconds in length. Repetition requests are focused on information necessary for the task in lines 2, 5 and 7. In line 8 the confirmation check is focused on establishing whether or not a particular subsection of the task has been accomplished.

(Seedhouse 1999: 151–152)

Seedhouse claims that this is very typical of TBI in his data. In his view, this form of interaction is potentially problematic, because it places severe constraints on the kinds of turn-taking roles each of the two learners in this task can play: 'the nature of the task pushes LI to make statements to which L2 will provide feedback, clarification, repetition requests, or repair initiation' (p.152). While conceding that this may be very useful for students who are studying a foreign language in order to communicate effectively in workplace contexts (where the giving and receiving of instructions may be a commonplace activity), Seedhouse points out that there are many other kinds of interaction in the world outside the classroom, and that most students will therefore need adequate practice in a much wider range of turn-taking roles than they would receive in a strongly task-based syllabus if they are to learn to communicate successfully in a foreign language.

The second concern that Seedhouse raises about TBI is that it may lead students to use the *features* of the target language in a way that is just as narrowly constrained as the turn-taking pattern discussed above. As illustration of this, Seedhouse (1999) presents the extract shown in Box 9.2.

Box 9.2: Extract 2 from Seedhouse (1999).

---

1 **LI:** Ready?
2 **L2:** Ready
3 **LI:** Er the blue oblong above the red oblong—eh! the yellow oblong.
4 **L2:** Alright. Faster, faster.
5 **LI:** The red cylinder beside the blue oblong.
6 **L2:** Left or right?
7 **LI:** Right.
8 **L2:** Right! ... OK.
9 **LI:** The the red cube was =
10 **L2:** = The red cube
11 **LI:** The red cube was behind the blue oblong.
12 **L2:** Blue oblong, blue oblong. Yeah.
13 **LI:** And the red cube was behind the red oblong.

This text certainly bears out Seedhouse's previous claim about the particular interaction pattern promoted by TBI; once again, we see that the turn taking roles adopted by the learners are being strongly constrained by the demands of the task. All L1 has to do is provide information in a repetitive format (lines 3, 5, 7, 9, 11 and 13), together with occasional checks to establish that L2 is keeping up (lines 1 and 7). Similarly, all L2 has to do is manage this flow of information, by confirming that he or she is ready to go on (lines 2 and 4, "OK" in line 8, and "Yeah" in line 12), or by getting L1 to slow down ("The red cube" in line 10) or pause for a moment ("Blue oblong, blue oblong" in line 12). However, Seedhouse's analysis of this text focuses not on its turn-taking structure but on its linguistic features. In particular, Seedhouse suggests that this text is typical of TBI in that it features a high degree of what he calls *indexicality* and *minimalization*.

'Indexicality' is the extent to which the meanings in a text are dependent on a knowledge of the context in which the text is being constructed. In other words, indexicality refers to the level of explicitness in a text. As a general rule, informal spoken language tends to be more indexical or 'context-dependent' than formal written language. This is particularly true when the speakers are in the same physical space together, and can therefore refer to the world around them in a very inexplicit way. In linguistic terms, high indexicality is evidenced by a greater use of pronominal forms of reference (e.g. 'Could you pass *it* over here?' instead of 'Could you pass *the book* over here?') and a higher incidence of unfinished statements. For example, instead of asking 'Could you pass the book/it over here?', you could ask someone to pass you a book simply by leaning towards it with arm outstretched, then looking at the other person (who we will assume is closer to the book than you are!) and saying 'Could you…?'. In these terms, the extracts in Boxes 9.1 and 9.2 are clearly highly indexical: they would have been virtually impossible for you to understand if we had not provided you with detailed background information explaining what is going on in each case.

By 'minimalization' Seedhouse means that '[t]here is a general tendency to minimize the volume of language used, and to produce only that which is necessary to accomplish the task. Turns tend to be relatively short, with simple syntactic constructions' (1999: 153). Seedhouse also notes that some grammatical features may even be omitted altogether if they are not found to be essential to the successful completion of the task. In Box 9.2, for example, the copular verb *be* is missing from lines 3 and 5. That is, L2 should have said 'The blue oblong **is** above the red oblong' and 'The red cylinder **is** beside the blue oblong', instead of 'The blue oblong above the red oblong' and 'The red cylinder beside the blue oblong'. Note also that in lines 9, 11 and 13, where L2 does remember to include a copula, the student has incorrectly used the past tense. As can be seen, however, these errors and omissions do not in any way impede the students as they work their way through the task; in fact, the students do not at any point talk about these errors (or 'orient themselves towards' these errors, in conversation analysis terms), which suggests that they may not even be aware of them at all.

Once again, this may be very useful practice for students in some contexts. It would, for example, help students to get a job done with maximum speed and efficiency in a factory or on an oilrig where English happened to be the medium of communication. But is it going to help learners to improve the accuracy or sophistication of their foreign language skills in more general terms? Proponents of TBI claim that engagement with pedagogic tasks pushes students to use their language to the limit, thereby promoting the acquisition of new forms via a process often referred to as interlanguage stretching. However, Seedhouse argues that 'what we often find in practice in task-based interaction is more or less the opposite process, with the learners producing such a minimum display of their linguistic competence that it resembles a pidgin' (1999: 154).

As well as the two practical pedagogic problems discussed above, Seedhouse also suggests that his analysis reveals a problem of a more theoretical nature. Specifically, he argues that it casts doubt on TBI's much vaunted second language acquisition (SLA) research credentials. Specifically, Seedhouse argues that SLA research on TBI is biased and circular because it is based on the quantitative analysis of precisely those features that TBI tends to produce a lot of: clarification requests, confirmation checks, comprehension checks and self-repetitions. Seedhouse uses this observation to make the more general point that SLA research – which tends to prefer experimental and quantitative methodologies – needs to make more extensive use of qualitative approaches to the analysis of classroom data such as that carried out in his own research.

An example of values analysis

In this section we will look in detail at an example of how applied linguists study texts in order to identify the sets of conventionalised meanings and values associated with them. Our case study is a comparative analysis of three undergraduate academic textbooks carried out by Australian applied linguist Tim Moore (2002). As is well known, the explicit purpose of the undergraduate textbook is to provide students with a thorough grounding in the fundamental concepts of their fields of study. In this study, however, Moore pursues the more interesting idea that textbooks may also serve a *normative* function, by imposing on their readers a very particular and partial view of what their field of studies is like – one that reflects the biases and preferences of the authors of the textbooks themselves, and which may in some cases downplay or even exclude possible alternative approaches to the academic subject area in question.

In testing this hypothesis Moore draws substantially on systemic-functional linguistics (Halliday and Matthiesen 2004; henceforth SFL). There are several reasons why SFL is an appropriate choice of approach for Moore's research. First of all, it is a social rather than a psychological theory of language. In other words, it views language as shaping and being shaped by human social interaction, and is not concerned with questions of how language develops and is stored and processed in the individual human mind. Second, SFL places meaning at the centre of analysis; in Halliday's terms, it provides a 'meaning-centred' rather than a 'form-centred' approach to linguistic description. Above all, SFL fits in very strongly with Moore's concerns in that it sees every act of linguistic meaning-making as an act of interpretation. That is, whenever we talk or write about a phenomenon – that is, a thing, an event, a process or a state of affairs in the world around us – we choose to talk or write about it in a particular way. In so doing, we are also in effect choosing not to talk or write about it in other ways that the language might in principle make available to us. For example, if we describe a particular phenomenon in the following way:

They put up the tent in the middle of the afternoon

We are choosing to 'construe' this phenomenon in this way, and not in any of the following ways, or in any of the other ways that we might have chosen to construe it:

By 3 o'clock, the tent was up

The middle of the afternoon saw them attempting to wrestle the tent into an upright position

It only took a few short minutes for the tent to go up

It seemed to take them forever to get the tent up

(etc.)

In other words, the language we use does not simply reflect external reality, like a mirror. On the contrary, SFL proposes that our language choices actively construe phenomena in the world in particular ways, and these construals reflect our own immediate purposes, interests, goals and our broader and more deep-seated social norms and cultural values, just as much as they reflect what is actually going on in the external world around us.

These interests in the social, in meaning, and in construal all come together in the particular aspect of SFL that Moore bases his textbook analysis on, transitivity analysis. 'Transitivity' is the term that grammarians use when they are analysing 'who does what to whom' in a clause or sentence. In SFL, transitivity analysis makes a basic distinction between the participants in an action or a relationship, the processes that these participants perform, or which link them together, and the circumstances in which participants and processes occur. To illustrate, consider clause (1) below, and the example analysis that follows it:

(1) They arrived at the campsite in the middle of the afternoon

Participant	Process	Circumstance	Circumstance
They	arrived	at the campsite	in the middle of the afternoon

Of course, many other transitivity configurations are possible; for example, there is only one participant in (1), but there are often two, as in example (2) below:

(2) They put up the tent in the middle of the afternoon

Participant	Process	Participant	Circumstance
They	put up	the tent	in the middle of the afternoon

You may have noticed that the two SFL transitivity analyses above divide each clause up in much the same way that a traditional grammatical analysis would do. In fact, the only difference is in the way that each element has been labelled. Whereas the SFL analysis uses labels that emphasise the semantic function of each element, a traditional analysis would simply replace these with terms indicating the formal grammatical role that each element plays. Thus, a traditional analysis would relabel (1) as Subject – Predicate – Adverbial – Adverbial, and (2) as Subject – Predicate – Object – Adverbial. In fact, you might even feel that the traditional analysis of (2) is better than the SFL one, in that it distinguishes between 'They' as the element that performs the 'putting up' action in this clause, and 'the tent' as the element that is on the receiving end of this action. However, SFL also recognises these finer-grained distinctions, and has a very extensive – but still meaning-focused – set of descriptors to account for such differences. To illustrate, consider the following more detailed analysis of sentence (2):

Actor	Process: Material	Goal	Circumstance: Time
They	put up	the tent	in the middle of the afternoon

Note that as well as distinguishing between Actor and Goal as two distinct kinds of Participant, this analysis also establishes that 'put up' is a particular kind of Process – specifically, a 'Material' process, in which some form of manual physical activity is involved – and that 'in the middle of the afternoon' is a circumstantial element that indicates when the event in question takes place. This is important because processes (i.e. verbs in traditional grammar) clearly do not always describe material actions, nor do circumstances (i.e. adverbials in traditional grammar) always indicate points or periods of time. In (3) below, for example, SFL designates the process as Verbal rather than Material, and the Participant as a Sayer rather than an Actor:

(3) She said they put up the tent in the middle of the afternoon

Sayer	Process: Verbal	Verbiage
She	said	they put up the tent in the middle of the afternoon

Another important difference between sentences (2) and (3) above is that while (2) is construing a phenomenon in the external world, (3) is not. Instead, (3) is *construing someone else's construal* of a phenomenon, by fronting it with the clause 'She said'. Furthermore, this 'projecting' clause (as it is termed in SFL) also has the effect of explicitly presenting the statement 'they put up the tent in the middle of the afternoon' not as an objective fact about the world, but as a subjective claim that other people may or may not agree with. Halliday (1994: 250) refers to these 'construals of construals' as *metaphenomena*, and notes that while they can take a variety of forms, they are most commonly found in the form of a *that*- clause preceded by a Verbal process such as 'say', 'argue' or 'claim', or a Mental process such as 'believe', 'think' or 'suppose'.

It is at this point that we come to Moore's study. Moore (2002) begins by reviewing a number of previous studies of scientific writing, which say that metaphenomenal statements are more strongly associated with research articles, while phenomenal statements (i.e. non-projected statements of 'fact') are more strongly associated with textbooks. According to this previous research, these associations are entirely appropriate, because they reflect the different purposes of these two types of text. Metaphenomenal statements are more common in research articles because it is in research articles that new and potentially contentious knowledge claims are first put forward. Similarly, phenomenal statements are more frequent in undergraduate textbooks because the principal role of textbooks is to present students in a given field with 'the facts' about a discipline: information, ideas and concepts that are universally agreed among experts in that field, and which thus constitute its essential foundations.

The aim of Moore's study was not to test both of these claims directly, but to investigate whether metaphenomenal discourse occurs equally frequently (or infrequently) in textbooks in a range of different subject areas. This was done by means of a comprehensive quantitative and qualitative text analysis of three 10,000-word samples taken from undergraduate textbooks in the academic disciplines of physics, economics and sociology respectively. Moore carried out this analysis by manually identifying and recording all of the metaphenomenal processes and participants in his three samples, and tabulating the results. It is worth noting that Moore's analysis took into account instances where metaphenomenal processes were expressed by nouns, as in example (4) below, as well as the more familiar cases where metaphenomenal processes were expressed by verbs, as in (5). (Note also that metaphenomenal processes are indicated by **bold** typeface, and metaphenomenal participants are indicated by CAPITALS.)

(4) From a MARXIAN **view**, systems of stratification derive from the relationship of social groups to the forces of production.

(5) NEWTON'S FIRST LAW **states** that: Every object continues in a state of rest or of uniform motion in a straight line, unless it is compelled to change that state by forces acting upon it.

A summary of Moore's quantitative findings is given in Table 9.1. As can be seen, Moore found considerable variation in the frequency of both metaphenomenal processes and participants across the three textbook samples studied in his research. The most obvious observation to be made about these findings is that metaphenomenal discourse is much more common in the sociology textbook than it is in the other two textbooks. While this finding certainly looks dramatic in itself, Moore suggests that it is actually very much in line with standard views of sociology as a highly contentious and factionalised academic discipline. There is no single dominant view among sociologists about how the social world is to be theorised or how sociological research should be carried out, and the claims that sociologists make will always remain claims, since they are based on interpretations rather than on experiments or calculations in which ideas can be proved to be true or false. It is therefore not surprising to find that statements in the sociology textbook are more likely to be presented metaphenomenally, that is, as claims to be debated, rather than as facts to be accepted.

Essentially the same points in reverse can be made about the observation that metaphenomenal discourse is much less frequent in the physics textbook than it is in the sociology textbook. Although debate and disagreement are just as much part and parcel of physics as they are of sociology (or any other discipline, for that matter), physicists differ from sociologists in that they share a common set of basic assumptions about the nature of the physical world, and about how to study it. Statements about the physical world that start off as controversial claims end up as accepted facts once a consensus has formed around them, and the process of knowledge creation is conceptualised as a series of problems which it is the goal of physics to solve, one by one, until the entire workings of the physical world are fully understood. In short, physicists see themselves as working together on a shared project, using essentially the same methods to arrive at shared goals, and it is thus appropriate that an introductory textbook in physics should present the discipline in these consensual and collegial terms.

Table 9.1 Frequency of metaphenomenal processes and participants in three academic textbook samples.

	Sociology	Physics	Economics
Metaphenomenal process verbs	252	105	55
Metaphenomenal process nouns	130	95	31
Metaphenomenal participants	225	51	23

Source: Moore 2002.

Much more surprising is the finding that metaphenomenal discourse is even less frequent in the economics textbook than it is in the physics textbook. Economics is usually classified as a social science rather than a physical science, and as such would be expected to show a closer affinity with sociology than it does with physics. However, the results of Moore's study suggest that the authors of this textbook want to present economics as a 'scientific', objective subject like physics, rather than as a 'humanistic', interpretative subject like sociology.

This observation is also borne out by the principal findings of Moore's qualitative analysis of metaphenomenal processes, a summary of which is presented in Table 9.2. Moore (2002: 354) points out that the most frequent metaphenomenal processes in sociology are all 'what might be called verbs of "assertion"'—that is, they are 'concerned with the asserting of certain "arguable" propositions'. Indeed, as example (6) below shows, even the most uncontroversial statements in sociology are often presented as assertions that could in principle be disputed:

(6) MOST SOCIOLOGISTS **argue** that systems of racial stratification have a social rather than a biological basis.

143

In physics and economics, in contrast, when metaphenomenal processes do occur, they hardly ever express debatable assertions; instead, they are used to present standard terms, concepts and definitions to the reader, as in examples (7) and (8) below:

(7) By convention, WE **call** national product gross domestic product (GDP) and national income gross national product (GNP). (Economics)

(8) The first law leads US to **define** an inertial co-ordinate system or reference system as one which Newton's first law holds true. (Physics)

Drawing once again on the terminology of SFL, Moore defines these as processes of 'signification', and argues that the function of such processes is 'not to project propositions around which there may be some disciplinary debate; rather it is to "conventionalise" certain modes of thinking, ones that a disciplinary novice is more or less required to accept.'

Table 9.2 **Most frequent metaphenomenal processes in Moore's data.[1]**

	Sociology	Physics	Economics
Verbs	argue (49)	define (12)	call (10)
	see (23)	represent (7)	say (5)
	suggest (14)	state (7)	represent (4)
	believe (12)	find (6)	conclude (3)
	claim (8)	refer (6)	define (3)
Nouns	view (18)	law (50)	concept (7)
	theory (13)	definition (7)	definition (5)
	perspective (9)	statement (7)	model (5)
	question (6)	procedure (5)	abbreviation (3)
	criticism (6)	equation (4)	distinction (3)

Note

1 Raw frequencies in brackets.

While Moore's analysis is entirely plausible in itself, you may have noticed that there is a potential problem with the distinction that he makes between processes of assertion (such as *argue, believe* and *claim*) and processes of signification (such as *define, call* and *represent*). This problem is that processes of signification cannot be clearly associated with 'facts', in the same way that processes of assertion can clearly be associated with 'claims'. For example, if we rephrase example (8) above as 'The first law leads SOME PHYSICISTS to **define** an inertial co-ordinate system or reference system as one which Newton's first law holds true', it is no longer being presented as a conventional definition that all physicists agree with, and that students are 'more or less required to accept'. Instead, we are now presenting it to students as a definition that some physicists accept, but which may not be accepted or used by others, and which must therefore be treated with some caution.

It is for this reason that Moore's analysis also takes metaphenomenal participants – the people who are doing the representing – into consideration. Following a process of categorisation similar to that used in Ädel's research (as discussed in Chapter 6), Moore finds that the metaphenomenal participants in his three textbook samples can be divided into three main types: 'individual scholars' (e.g. Marx, Keynes, Newton), 'schools of thought' (e.g. Marxist, Functionalist, Newtonian), and 'generic scholars' (e.g. 'some sociologists', 'researchers', 'we'). As can be seen in Table 9.3, metaphenomenal participants are much more frequent in sociology than they are in the other two textbooks, with the 'individual scholars' category accounting for 75 per cent of all instances. This supports Moore's general argument that the sociology textbook represents sociology as a very contentious and argument-driven field of studies, in which there are comparatively few areas of agreement and consensus. Conversely, the discipline of physics is presented as highly stable and consensus-driven, and the relative absence of metaphenomenal discourse suggests that the physics textbook is primarily concerned with teaching students facts rather than claims about the physical world, and about how physicists go about studying it. And once again, Moore finds the economics textbook attempting to present economics as an even more scientific discipline than physics.

145

Table 9.3 **Quantitative overview of metaphenomenal participants in Moore's data.**

	Sociology	Physics	Economics
Individual scholars	169	7	4
Schools of thought	36	29	0
Generic scholars	20	15	19
TOTALS	225	51	23

Particularly striking in this regard is the comparatively high frequency of 'generic scholars' statements in the economics textbook, such as examples (9) and (10) below (see also 7 above):

(9)   ECONOMISTS **say** that neither output nor the price is in equilibrium when aggregate demand exceeds the current rate of production.

(10) WE have the following **conclusion**: the economy will reach an equilibrium at full employment only if the amount consumers wish to save is precisely equal to the amount that investors want to invest.

As Moore (2002: 357) observes,

> In the economics text, generic scholars are treated in all instances as a single collective group … By contrast, nowhere in the sociology text is there an attempt to depict a single collective voice in the discipline. All references to the generic sociologist are provided with some pre-modification — most sociologists, many sociologists, some sociologists, etc. as in (6) above.[1]

In short, although both sociology and economics are traditionally classified as social sciences, the two textbooks analysed by Moore seem to present very different conceptions of what each of these supposedly related disciplines is like.

But is there anything wrong with this? If economics is actually more like physics than it is like sociology, then it would be reasonable to argue that it is not the textbook that is at fault, but the traditional classification of academic disciplines itself. However, in the concluding section of his research paper Moore argues that this is very far from being the case. Reviewing a number of articles on the subject of economics education, Moore (2002: 359) reports that:

> A number of commentators have argued that the drive in economics to achieve a paradigmatic, scientific status has involved, among other things, a deliberate excluding of alternative positions and voices (Brown, 1993; Helburn, 1986). Helburn, for example, in her analysis of the state of economics education, speaks of the almost complete dominance of the 'Neoclassical/Keynsian synthesis', in spite of the existence of a diversity of minority dissident schools—New Classicals, post-Keynsians, neo-Keynsians, fundamentalist Marxists, structural Marxists, etc.—none of which, she says, receive any meaningful attention in university courses (see also Holt and Pressman, 1998). This absence of other disciplinary 'participants' was observed clearly in the sample economics text—in contrast to sociology, whose embrace of multiple voices was a defining feature of the text. Klamer (1990), also a critic, sees economics as a social science discipline, but one that has sought a spurious kind of legitimacy by aspiring to the standards and methods of the physical sciences. Thus, Klamer suggests, the subject has tended to 'make its textbooks in the image of physics textbooks', presenting a harmonious methodological and ideological picture of itself to the world. Such an observation goes some way to explaining the study's finding of such a strong positivist orientation in the economics text. In the discipline's desire for scientific credibility, it may be that some economics texts are made to appear more physics-like than physics itself.

By identifying and quantifying instances of metaphenomenal discourse in his textbook samples, then, Moore was able to corroborate these criticisms. In particular, it does seem to be the case that the economics textbook studied by Moore (which was the set textbook for first year undergraduates at the university where Moore himself was working) imposes on students a very narrow and biased view of what their field of study is like. Interestingly, Moore concludes by proposing that his own applied linguistic analysis – and the concept of metadiscourse that underpins it – may help to counter the dominance of the 'neoclassical' orthodoxy as embodied in the textbook:

> The critics of economics education have been quite fervent in their calls for reform in the discipline, especially in relation to how the discipline is constructed discursively for its students. … Brown (1993) speaks of the need for a 'decanonizing discourse', one that would 'construct a space for a greater range of voices to be heard within the history of economic thought' (p.78). Klamer calls for texts that convey a sense of the subject as 'discourse and conversation' (1990, p. 153), and Helburn for texts that 'imbue some sense of the relativeness of knowledge and the legitimacy of different and conflicting viewpoints' (1986, p. 7). The term 'metaphenomenon' is a rather technical one, and probably unfamiliar outside the field of linguistics— but this would seem to be a useful way of characterising the type of discourse so eagerly sought.

(Moore 2002: 359)

Problems with text analysis

Text analysis is one of the most powerful and popular research approaches in applied linguistics. As with all approaches, however, it is not without its own problems and limitations. One of the most widely acknowledged of these problems concerns what is often referred to as the subjectivity of text analysis. No matter how rigorously it is carried out, text analysis is fundamentally an act of interpretation. This inevitably raises the possibility that different analysts might interpret the same data in very different ways – which in turn raises the question of how we can evaluate the plausibility or cogency of any particular analysis.

One way of addressing this problem is to incorporate some form of inter-rater reliability testing into the analysis itself. This procedure requires all data to be analysed separately by two or more analysts. The analysts then compare their analyses in order to make sure that they have made the same decisions and are thus seeing 'the same' categories in the data. In practice, however, many if not most text analysis projects (and virtually all student assignments) are carried out by lone researchers who do not have the time or resources to carry out any inter-rater reliability testing procedures. In itself, this is not necessarily regarded as a problem in applied linguistics, as long as the reader is provided with a very clear account of the analytical framework used in the research, of how the analysis was carried out, and on what basis particular coding decisions were made. Alternatively, some other researchers (and postmodernist researchers in particular) circumvent the problem by explicitly acknowledging the highly subjective and interpretative nature not only of their analysis, but of all forms of analysis. In effect, the argument is not so much 'if you used this analytical framework you would obtain the same results as I did' as 'this is how I understand the data, but you may read it differently'.

The other problem that we want to flag up here is one that affects both of the sample analyses reviewed in detail above. Both Seedhouse (1999) and Moore (2002) make very general claims – about task-based learning and academic textbooks respectively – on the basis of close and detailed analyses of comparatively small amounts of textual data. Of course, 'small' is to a certain extent in the eye of the beholder; Seedhouse's conclusions are based on conversation analyses of over 300 lesson transcripts, while Moore's arguments rest on a comprehensive analysis of 30,000 words of written text. Both of these analyses will have been extremely time-consuming and arduous; indeed it would be unreasonable to expect either analyst to have done more. It is also worth noting that there is a very good tradition of trust in applied linguistics; we assume that researchers are telling us the truth about their data. Thus, when Seedhouse (1999: 151) says that Box 1 'is typical of the interaction which resulted from this task', we accept that this is actually the case.

Nevertheless, we are still left with the question of how representative these analyses actually are of the wider phenomena that each researcher wants to make claims about. It is noticeable, for instance, that all of the examples of TBI in Seedhouse (1999) are information gap tasks. How typical is this type of task of task-based language teaching in general? And when Seedhouse says '[w]hat we also often find in practice in task-based interaction is a tendency to produce very indexical interaction' (p. 153), it is difficult for the reader not to wonder how often 'often' is. Similar questions can be posed about Moore's (2002) study. How representative are 10,000-word samples of textbooks each of which probably runs to 100,000 words or more? And how representative of textbooks in general are the three individual textbooks chosen for analysis in Moore's research? Moore's solution to the latter of these two problems is to adopt the commonly used (and very common sense) strategy of asking specialists in each of the three fields to recommend textbooks that are in their view representative of their kind, either because they are commonly used or because they are highly regarded by experts such as themselves. But clearly this is a compromise rather than a comprehensive solution to this particular problem, and in an ideal world analyses such as Seedhouse's and Moore's would be carried out on much larger sets of data. Until recently, this was simply not possible. Now, however, this situation is changing rapidly, thanks to advances in computer technology that will form the main focus of the next chapter of this book.

Conclusion

We began this chapter by setting out what texts are and why they are of interest to applied linguists. We then considered how the concept of 'text analysis' relates to (and differs from) the concept of 'discourse analysis' with which it is often confused. We then looked in detail at two very different approaches to text analytic work; one based on the essentially inductive methodology of conversation analysis, and the other based on the essentially deductive methodology of systemic-functional linguistics. We concluded by identifying some of the perennial problems that face any researcher who wants to do text analytic work. In the following chapter we will look at a range of new techniques that promise to substantially ameliorate, if not entirely solve, some of these methodological problems.

Analysing corpora

Introduction

As mentioned in the previous chapter, it is now increasingly common for applied linguists to work with large databases of texts stored on computer hard drives or websites and accessed electronically via specialist software. In this chapter we focus on this *corpus-based* approach to linguistic analysis. The chapter begins by looking in more detail at what a computer corpus is, and how to go about choosing or building one in order to answer applied linguistic research questions. We then look at some of the new ways of looking at language that electronic corpora and corpus analysis software have made possible, and review some of the many exciting ways in which applied linguists are using these new tools and resources. We will conclude by providing an example of how text analysis and corpus analysis can be combined fruitfully.

What is a corpus?

John Sinclair, one of the founders of modern corpus linguistics, defines a corpus as 'a collection of naturally-occurring language text, chosen to characterize a state or variety of a language' (Sinclair 1991: 171). This is a good starting point, but there are a number of additions, qualifications and refinements that we need to make to this definition in order to make it fully adequate for our purposes. First, and as mentioned above, we need to note that the term 'corpus' nowadays generally implies a text collection that is stored and accessed on a computer. Until fairly recently, applied linguists would commonly refer to any collection of attested language data as a corpus. Nowadays, however, this term is becoming so strongly associated with electronic text databases that researchers who work with collections of non-computerised field notes or photocopied texts are more likely to talk about 'my data' than 'my corpus', in order to avoid confusing their readers about the kind of analysis they are doing.

Second, we need to add that the term 'corpus' in applied linguistics is nowadays generally reserved for text collections that are very large. It is not possible to put an exact figure on how large 'very large' is, but a good rule of thumb would be to say that a text collection can be described as a corpus if it is too big for a researcher to perform a manual analysis on it. Indeed, as we will see later in this chapter, this is precisely the appeal of corpus linguistics: it allows the researcher to study language data on a scale and in ways that would simply have been unthinkable before the advent of modern computer technology.

Third, we need to expand a little on Sinclair's notion of 'naturally-occurring language'. By this term Sinclair means language that has been generated by real speakers and writers in real communicative contexts, rather than language that has been invented solely for the purposes of linguistic analysis or argumentation, such as Chomsky's famous sentence 'Colourless green ideas sleep furiously'. (This sentence was generated in order to show that grammaticality judgements can be made about meaningless sentences, and thus to support Chomsky's claim that syntax is independent of semantics.) Whereas theoretical linguists tend to be interested in what is *possible* in language, corpus linguists are interested in studying what is *typical*; they are interested in finding out what people usually say and write in order to make meanings in the course of their daily lives. As a result, data that are not **attested** instances of usage are not considered to be useful or valid for corpus linguistic analysis – unless, of course, you wanted to do a corpus study of the invented sentences that generative grammarians concoct in their research papers!

Finally, it is worth observing that the definition above talks about 'naturally-occurring language text', and not about 'naturally-occurring language texts' or 'naturally-occurring language samples'. This is because both approaches to corpus building are possible in corpus linguistics:

there are corpora that consist of collections of whole texts, and there are corpora that consist of collections of samples taken from whole texts. While the relative merits of whole-text or sample-based collection policies are a matter of ongoing debate among corpus linguists, it is fair to say that most applied linguists who work with corpora tend to favour the whole-text approach.

Types of corpus

Nowadays, corpora come in a wide variety of shapes and sizes. As a general rule, the largest corpora available today tend to be general corpora, which are designed in order to be representative of a language as a whole. Examples of English general corpora include the 100-million-word British National Corpus and the 450-million word Bank of English (BoE). Although there are more general corpora of English than there are for any other language, there are now general corpora representing many other major languages; examples include CREA for Spanish, COSMAS for German, the LCMC for Mandarin Chinese and the PNC for Polish. Many if not most general corpora are usually divided into more specific subcorpora, which can also be studied in their own right. For example, if you are interested in comparing the language of 'quality' and 'tabloid' newspapers, or of newspapers of different political persuasions, the BoE has a substantial collection of newspaper data divided up into individual publications, making it possible for you to make such comparisons. Similarly, if you wanted to focus exclusively on a particular feature as it occurs in spoken English, the BNC includes a subcorpus of 10 million words of spoken data that can be studied independently of the 90 million words of written data that comprise the remainder of the corpus.

Subcorpora within general language corpora overlap substantially with the next type of corpus to be identified here, specialised corpora. As the name suggests, specialised corpora are corpora that have been compiled with the explicit goal of representing a particular variety or subset of a language. Examples include CHILDES, a corpus of parent-child interactions; ICLE, a learner corpus consisting of essays written by EFL students from 14 different first language backgrounds; MICASE, a corpus of spoken academic English recorded at a university in the United States; and the TIME corpus, which consists of issues of the famous American news magazine of that name. The TIME corpus is also noteworthy in that it spans a period of 100 years. This makes it an example of a diachronic corpus, in contrast to synchronic corpora such as the BNC, which aim to represent a language or language variety at just one particular point or period in time. Another variant form in this regard is the monitor corpus, which is a corpus that is constantly being updated; new material is regularly added, and older material is regularly discarded. The Bank of English is an example of such a corpus. Monitor corpora are particularly useful for lexicography, where it is particularly important for users to have an accurate picture of current usage. Finally, it is worth noting that the advent of the Internet has made it very easy for researchers to compile corpora of their own on an ad hoc basis, simply by copying and pasting documents into plain text files stored on their own computer hard drives. The legal status of such DIY corpora is highly dubious, however, and researchers who compile such resources for their own research projects should still attempt to obtain permissions from copyright holders wherever possible, and must not distribute the corpora that they have collected to others.

Accessing and choosing corpora

Although more and more corpora are now being compiled around the world, the availability of these resources varies considerably. Corpora that have been created under the auspices of funded academic research projects tend to be freely available to anyone who wishes to use them; usually, the only stipulation is that you need to agree to a set of terms and conditions stating that you will use the corpus for academic research only, and not for any commercial purposes. Examples of such corpora include the British Academic Written English Corpus, the VU Amsterdam Metaphor Corpus, and The Lancaster Corpus of Mandarin Chinese, all of which (together with many other resources) are downloadable from the excellent and easy-to-use Oxford Text Archive web portal.[1] Other corpora are publicly available via specially designed websites hosted at individual institutions; leading examples of these include the resources hosted at the University of Michigan English Language Institute,[2] and the resources provided by Professor Mark Davies at Brigham Young University.[3] Corpora whose construction has been at least partially funded by publishers or other commercial organisations, such as the Bank of English, tend to be available via paid subscription only, while other such resources (those maintained and developed by Cambridge University Press being a particularly tantalising example) are not currently available to the general public at all. An interesting alternative to subscription-based access to individual corpora is now provided by an Internet resource called Sketch Engine.[4] Subscribing to this service provides the user with access to a wide range of corpora in many different languages, and a tool that automatically compiles 'customised' corpora from webpages.

Given the increasingly wide range of corpora now available for research purposes, it is worth pausing for a moment to think about what issues might be involved in choosing a corpus for analysis. On this issue, perhaps the most useful point to bear in mind is that 'a corpus is neither good nor bad in itself, but suited or not suited to a particular purpose' (Hunston 2002: 26). In other words, your choice of corpus will depend to a very great extent on what you are interested in. This is largely a matter of common sense; you would not use a spoken corpus to investigate written language, nor would you base your arguments about verb tense preferences in Singaporean English on a corpus of Australian newspaper articles. But it is also important to bear in mind other less immediately obvious issues and limitations, such as when a corpus was compiled. For example, the BNC will be of no use to you if you want to study how language has been affected by the rise of new communications technologies; it was compiled in the 1980s, and therefore contains no mention of recent Internet phenomena such as blogs, eBay or Facebook. In short, if you are going to use an existing corpus, be a critical consumer – read the small print! And if you are compiling your own, you need to make sure that the texts you have chosen are informed by clear and cogent set of design principles, and do your best to compile a corpus that not only allows you to make claims about the group or language you want to, but also will support the kinds of analysis you plan to do.

Corpus analysis methods

Obviously, the only way to study very large corpora of texts held on computer is via specialist corpus analysis software. In the past, this basic technical requirement meant that corpus linguistics was the sole preserve of a small group of (usually very technically-minded) researchers. More recently, however, a wide range of powerful but user-friendly software packages and web-based resources have become available to the novice or casual user, and corpus analysis now sits very firmly within the mainstream of applied linguistics methodologies. In this section we will describe some of the capabilities of these modern software resources, focusing in particular on techniques that are now well known and widely used in applied linguistics. We are not going to explain how these techniques are carried out on any one particular web interface or piece of standalone software, however. Software changes quickly and may or may not be available for particular operating systems. Web interfaces are even more idiosyncratic, and are usually more restricted in their functionality than most standalone software packages are. If you want to know exactly how a particular type of analysis is carried out on a particular piece of software, then we suggest you read the online manual or 'Readme' file that comes with the software, or ask someone who already knows how to use the software to help you get started.

Counting and listing words

Consider again the brief definition with which we began this chapter:

> A corpus is a collection of naturally-occurring language text, chosen to characterize a state or variety of a language.

How many words are there in that sentence? For a corpus linguist, this question has two answers. If by 'words' we mean word tokens (i.e. the number of running words in the sentence), the answer is 20, assuming that the hyphenated string 'naturally-occurring' counts as two words rather than one. If on the other hand we mean word types (i.e. the number of different words in the sentence), then you should find that the answer is 15, as follows: *a, corpus, is, collection, of, naturally, occurring, language, text, chosen, to, characterize, state, or, variety*. You should also have found that while it will only have taken you between seven and ten seconds to count the number of word tokens in the sentence, it will have taken you rather longer to calculate the number of word types – and that you might even have got it slightly wrong as well. (Perhaps you only counted 'a' three times instead of four, or – as we did the first time we tried this ourselves – counted 'language' as a new word twice!) In less than the time it took you to do either of these calculations, a piece of corpus analysis software would be able to calculate the number of word types and word tokens in a whole text, or indeed in a corpus containing hundreds or even thousands of texts. It would also be able to provide you with a list of all the word types arranged in frequency order, like this:

Rank	Freq.	Word
1	4	a
2	2	language
3	2	of
4	1	characterize
5	1	chosen
6	1	collection
7	1	corpus
8	1	is
9	1	naturally
10	1	occurring
11	1	or
12	1	state
13	1	text
14	1	to
15	1	variety

The software will probably also allow you to arrange your word frequency list in various other ways: in reverse frequency order, in alphabetical order, or even in reverse alphabetical order – which is very useful if you want to study words ending in -tion, -ing or -ty, for example.

Although sometimes dismissed by more qualitatively-oriented linguists as mere 'bean-counting', frequency profiling techniques such as these have had a revolutionary impact on a range of subfields within applied linguistics. To take just one example, they have allowed researchers in the fields of second language vocabulary acquisition and second language reading to establish relationships between levels of vocabulary knowledge and levels of reading comprehension among learners of English as a foreign language. These researchers have found that, while knowledge of the top 2,000 most frequent words in the English language will provide a learner with 80 per cent coverage of a typical unsimplified English text, the learner will need to have acquired a receptive vocabulary of around 10,000 words in order to reach the 95 per cent threshold that is generally thought to be the point at which it is possible to engage fully with the meaning of such a text.

The ability to calculate word types and tokens automatically has also had a profound effect on fields such as stylistics and forensic linguistics, where type/token ratios (TTR) are used to determine shifts in the style, readability or even possible authorship of a text. TTR is also a standard measurement in speech therapy and clinical linguistics, where it is used to study vocabulary development patterns and word retrieval problems in children with learning difficulties and adults who have suffered brain injuries.

Another important observation arising from word frequency lists is that a very large proportion (often as much as 50 per cent of a corpus) consists of words that occur only once in that corpus. Corpus linguists call these one-off words *hapax legomena*, or 'hapaxes' for short. What is important about this observation is that it helps to explain why corpora need to be big: most words – even so-called 'common' words, like 'write' or 'table' – occur only very infrequently in attested language data, so a large corpus is necessary in order to make statements about all but the most frequently occurring items in a language.

Studying relationships between words

All words form relationships with other words, and it has long been recognised in linguistics that some words are more likely to occur together than others. Some of these co-occurrence relationships can be explained in traditional terms, as simple facts of grammar. The word *the*, for example, is related to the word *back* because *the* is a determiner and *back* is a noun, and we know that determiners very often precede nouns in sentences. However corpus linguistics also makes it possible to study co-occurrences between words that cannot be explained by traditional grammar. These lexical co-occurrences are called *collocations*.

The term 'collocation' has a special meaning in corpus linguistics; formally, it is the tendency for certain words to occur significantly frequently within a given physical span (i.e. number of words) to the left or right of a central or node word. This is very different from some other areas of linguistics, in which the term 'collocation' refers to a type of semi-fixed phrase. For example, the whole phrase 'make a mistake' would be described as a collocation by some linguists, but in corpus analysis we would say that 'make' and 'a' are collocates of the node word 'mistake', or that 'a' and 'mistake' are collocates of 'make' (or even that 'make' and 'mistake' are collocates of 'a', if the results of our analysis tell us that this is the case).

The simplest way of identifying collocations in a corpus is simply to count their raw frequencies; that is, the more frequently a word occurs in the vicinity of another word, the more confident we can be in saying that it is a collocate of that word. The problem with this approach is that we often get an unmanageably long list of collocates, and many of the words at the top of our list will only be there for fairly obvious grammatical reasons. This is why many corpus linguists prefer to use lists of collocations that are based on statistical significance scores calculated by the computer. The purpose of these tests is to 'filter out' collocates that are there simply because they occur frequently in general, and to leave the researcher with a list of words that are particularly strongly associated with the node word under analysis. To illustrate this, consider Table 10.1, which presents two different lists of the top ten collocates of the node word *eye* in the Bank of English. On the left is the raw frequency list; on the right is a list ranked according to a statistical measure called t-score. (The numbers on the right in each column represent word frequencies and statistical significance scores respectively.)

Table 10.1 **Top ten raw frequency and t-score collocates of *eye* in the Bank of English.**

Rank	Raw frequency		t-score	
1	the	25930	an	72.343535
2	a	10519	on	51.803129
3	and	9613	keep	46.100750
4	to	9246	eye	41.865427
5	of	8292	his	40.156801
6	in	7400	the	39.473791
7	an	7357	caught	35.577521
8	on	6747	blind	33.750945
9	s	5537	catching	33.680444
10	with	4404	with	31.701478

As you can see, these two lists are very different. The raw frequency collocates present us with some hard facts about our data, but the problem is that these are all high frequency grammatical words such as *the, and* and *of*, which will occur in the vicinity of any singular countable noun. The t-score list, in contrast, is much more interesting, and seems to tell us more about the linguistic behaviour of *eye* in particular. Specifically, it identifies a number of words that go together with *eye* to make up a number of idiomatic phrases. The top three collocates give us the sequence *keep an eye on*; the fourth and tenth most significant collocates in this list are there because they participate in the phrase *see eye to eye with* [someone/something]; *his* is the most frequent of several possessive determiners that occur in the phrase *caught* [someone's] *eye*; a closer inspection of *blind* gives us *turn a blind eye to* [something]; and *catching* is part of the compound adjective *eye-catching*. Even the turns out to be a statistically significant (as well as the most frequently occurring) collocate of *eye*; this is at least partly due to the fact that it is a more or less mandatory element in many phrases. For example, native speakers almost always say *out of **the** corner of my/your/her/his eye*, and not *out of **a** corner of my/your/her/his eye*, or *out of **one** corner of my/your/her/his eye*, even though these alternatives are equally grammatically acceptable – or no less nonsensical, given that eyes do not actually have corners at all!

It should be clear from the above that statistical collocates provide a very powerful perspective on the phenomenon of collocation. However, it is also important to bear in mind at all times that statistical significance scores are artefacts of analysis – they are interpretations of the raw data, and not empirical facts about the data in themselves. It is also important to note that if you want to study collocation using statistical tests, you will almost certainly need a multi-million-word corpus. In a corpus of one million words or fewer, there may not be enough instances of your node word for the software to be able to decide what its significant collocates are. This is one of the main reasons why most corpus linguists agree with Sinclair's dictum that 'bigger is almost always better'.

Identifying multi-word units

As we have seen, identifying the statistical collocates of a word can help you to identify the frequent phrases in which that word appears. For example, we saw that the top three t-score collocates of *eye* in the BoE are *keep, and* and *on*, which in effect gave us most of the phrase *keep an eye on* (someone/something). But what if you could identify these phrases directly?

To a certain extent this is now possible, by asking the computer to search your corpus for strings of words of different lengths that occur above a certain level of frequency in your corpus. These strings are variously known in applied linguistics as *lexical bundles, n-grams, clusters, lexical phrases* and *formulaic sequences*, among many other terms, but we will call them *multi-word units* (or MWUs for short) here.

There are two main ways of identifying MWUs in corpus data. One is to ask the computer to identify all and any MWUs that contain one or more words that you specify yourself. For example, asking the computer to find all four-word and five-word MWUs containing the word *eye* might well yield such phrases as *keep an eye on, see eye to eye with* and *turn a blind eye to*. The other approach is to specify only the length of MWUs, and to leave the matter of what words actually occur in these strings entirely open. This may yield some very interesting results, but of course it will also yield a much larger dataset for you to sift through. It is for this reason that corpus linguists typically set quite a high cut-off point for such searches (e.g. telling the computer only to list MWUs that occur at least 15 or 20 times per million words of data).

This 'semi-automatic' approach to corpus analysis has become very popular in recent years, and is most strongly associated with the work of Douglas Biber and his colleagues (e.g. Biber *et al.* 1999). Among many other things, Biber and colleagues have shown that these sequences can be used as a crude but effective way of distinguishing between written and spoken registers. For example, they note that MWUs such as *I want you to, take a look at* and *it's going to be* are much more common in spoken English than they are in written English, while MWUs such as *as a result of, on the basis of* and *on the other hand* are much more strongly associated with written English than they are with spoken English.

The main limitation of this approach is that it is based on an algorithm (i.e. a computerised routine) that looks for exact repetitions of a given sequence. But many if not most of the idiomatic phrases that make up these sequences have one or more variable elements in them:

e.g. keep an eye on it/*them/you/her/him/them/John/the time/* ...

and/or can be transformed grammatically:

e.g. I'll *keep* an eye on it/I *kept* an eye on it/I've been *keeping* an eye on it and/or allow other words to intervene:

e.g. She kept a *watchful* eye on it

All of these variations have the effect of 'interrupting' the sequence, from the computer's point of view, and will therefore not be counted by the computer unless they themselves also occur very frequently – and even then the computer will fail to recognise that they are all variants of the same fundamental MWU, and will list them as separate units instead. There are techniques that you can use to compensate for this problem to some extent, and software is now getting better at identifying variable units such as these, but the fact remains that this is still very much a methodological problem which has yet to be fully solved.

Identifying keywords

As well as allowing researchers to identify and study relationships between words, corpus analysis also allows applied linguists to identify words that are particularly strongly associated with certain texts or corpora, and thus with the speakers and writers that these texts and corpora represent. This approach to analysis is known as keywords analysis. The usual approach to keywords analysis is to compare the corpus that the researcher is interested in (often called the node corpus) against a larger and more general reference corpus, which represents a notional norm of some kind. The software compares the frequency figures for all of the words in the research corpus with those of the same words in the reference corpus, and makes a list of any words which occur significantly more frequently in the research corpus than they do in the reference corpus.

Another variant on the keywords procedure is to compare two corpora of similar sizes in order to identify words that differentiate them from each other. A good example of this approach is a study by Gabrielatos and Baker (2008), which focused on the language used by the British press to talk about refugees, asylum seekers and immigrants to the UK. Gabrielatos and Baker used keywords analysis software to compare a corpus of articles on this topic published in 'tabloid' newspapers such as *The Sun* and *The Daily Mail* with a corpus of articles on the same topic published in 'quality' newspapers such as *The Times* and *The Guardian*.

Predictably, this analysis found that the tabloid newspapers characteristically represented refugees, asylum seekers and immigrants in negative and even hostile terms – as *cheats, crooks, fanatics* and *spongers* who are *flooding* into the country in order to make *bogus asylum claims* at the expense of UK *taxpayers*. Less predictably (and much less depressingly, from a liberal perspective at least), such terms were found to be significantly absent from the quality press corpus. Instead, many of the keywords associated with this corpus – *dissident, legitimacy, humanitarian, diversity* and the like – were found to be much more sympathetic, or at least neutral, towards refugees, asylum seekers and immigrants, and contributed to 'a more in-depth treatment of asylum/immigration issues, placed within a wider context (e.g. international, social, political, religious), with, arguably, more balanced argumentation' (Gabrielatos and Baker 2008: 30).

Most keywords are content rather than function words (and nouns in particular). But sometimes function words occur in keyword lists too, and are often more worthy of close analysis than they might at first seem. For example, Groom (2007) found the preposition *against* to be a keyword in a corpus of academic research articles in the field of history. As might be expected, this association is largely due to the prominence of accounts and analyses of conflict and oppression in historical discourse:

> Venice took no part in the war *against* the Normans

> extreme competition shaped policies that discriminated *against* blacks.

However, Groom found that *against* also collocates with the nouns *background* and *backdrop* in history, and plays an important function in linking historical events to particular circumstances:

> deliberation took place *against* a changing *backdrop* of military events

> Belgium's 'Europeanism' is similarly incomprehensible unless seen *against* the *background* of its internal dissensions

It is also worth noting at this point that the keywords procedure is not limited to single words, but can be extended to MWUs as well. A good example of this is a learner corpus study by Milton (1998), who found that his Cantonese L1 students of English for Academic Purposes overused stock phrases such as *in a nutshell* and *as we all know*, and underused MWUs found in native speaker academic writing, such as *an example of this* and *this is not to*. The practical implications of such work for syllabus and materials design are clear.

As with other corpus methods, keyword analysis has its own limitations, and there are caveats to consider when using it for certain purposes. In particular it is important to bear in mind the issue of comparability; for example, it would be a serious error to use the BNC as a means of generating keywords for a specialised corpus which consists in whole or in large part of North American texts. Doing this would almost certainly lead to words appearing simply because they are spelled differently in American English (e.g. *color*, *aluminum* and *gray*), and some verb forms might appear on account of differences between British and American English in terms of tense usage (e.g. 'I already did it' in American English versus 'I've already done it' in British English).

Studying language in co(n)text

Clearly, researchers cannot make much sense of the words or MWUs in a frequency or keywords list simply by looking at this list by itself – it is necessary to look at the items in such lists in context. This is where concordancing comes into play. Virtually all corpus analysis software includes a 'key word in context' (KWIC) concordancer, which allows the researcher to analyse a word or phrase in its typical context (or more accurately, its typical co-text) by placing it in the middle of the computer screen, as shown in Figure 10.1.

Of course this is not to imply that concordancing is only useful for contextualising the results of a wordlist or keyword analysis. On the contrary, concordancers were among the first corpus analysis tools to be developed, and remain the most widely used corpus analysis tool in applied linguistics. The appeal of the concordancer is that it allows you to sort data alphabetically to the right or the left. This in turn allows you to analyse your data more efficiently and to see otherwise hidden patterns within it. This leads us on to the key differences between text and corpus analysis, which, as Tognini-Bonelli (2001) points out, centre on the *direction* and *purpose* of reading. Text analysis involves reading individual texts one at a time; it is a linear process; and the analysis is typically complete and comprehensive. Corpus analysis, on the other hand, involves studying

```
           obvious. Ministers acknowledged the problem seven months later, when full
    had them? what do I THINK caused the problem? [p] [p] [h] What do I think can
              in the Gulf had complicated the problem. He said his country, which is due
       which have not yet encountered the problem should commence immediate
The select committee has exposed the problem. Now it is up to the Government to
                    solving; we have identified the problem; we know how the problem can be
      turned up. Nobody had noticed the problem with the spleen. The buffeting
             s life. Once you have raised the problem it becomes easier to find help.
          They thought they had solved the problem, but I wanted to show them the
            to 6x4 inch. So far I've solved the problem by having selectively cropped
    to resent them. She had solved the problem with Jason but realized she was
                 Mr. Merrill has studied the problem of same-sex violence in the gay
         the story went on) had talked the problem over with Dan McMichael of
  John's subconscious had solved the problem. It had given him extra time to
        worried vets, first spotlighted the problem that cows were catching a brain
```

Figure 10.1 [past participle]+the+problem in the Bank of English.

lots of texts all at once; the direction of reading is vertical, is focused on looking for patterns, and not all of the data is read or even seen as relevant.

Above all, the concordancer is the tool *par excellence* for revealing language features that are so large and so obvious that language learners and native speakers alike almost always fail to notice them. To illustrate this, try to answer the following question without looking at any corpus data: what is the difference between the plural nouns *factors* and *aspects*? When you have formulated an answer, look at Figures 10.2 and 10.3 below. What these concordances clearly show is that *factors* (but not *aspects*) tends to be preceded by adjectives, while *aspects* (but not *factors*) is nearly always followed by 'of', and then another noun. Did you include either of these observations in your own explanation?

165

```
                    pregnant) than to biological  factors. In one study, the frequency of
        <p> When people are affected by  factors like illness unemployment they can
                 1978, p. 121). Quite why class  factors exercised such a crucial influence
    placed on environmental and dietary  factors and encouraging women to have an
        issued a report showing that dietary  factors lead to breast cancer--
          will ultimately be decided by local  factors and largely invisible local
but, warns researcher Dr Alan Lucas,  factors such as family background may also
            the various positive and negative  factors that affect sexual desire as three-
           grades are only one of a range of  factors taken into account by Course
                      point to a variety of  factors behind the trend, including
              is determined by a number of  factors, such as your occupation age, sex,
       job their position all those kind of  factors which are so upsetting for people
     prepared to take? This depends on  factors such as your personality, how much
            There have been several other  factors involved in Celtic's recent slump,
     and identifying the precipitating  factors in migraine described above, it is
     treatment. Reviews of psychosocial  factors that can affect the impact of
          or without regard to relevant  factors; of if the evidence relied on by
     methods of early detection. <h> Risk  factors </h> <p> The first step in
            lack of fitness is one of several  factors causing heart disease -- there are
     role of consciousness and spiritual  factors in health and illness, which many
          simply a result of such subjective  factors as others' stereotypes,
     REP: And those are just some of the  factors which result in more than one in
              to demand and supply. All the  factors of production are privately owned,
   have done so much to transform the  factors we know." <p> Flynn's researches,
to women. One reason may be that the  factors which are thought to influence the
        from some combination of these  factors, although of them all, open
   larger families, but even when these  factors were screened out dummy use was
        men found that all the traditional  factors linked to male infertility-saunas,
            right now? Consider the underlying  factors that may be influencing you.
          and how you manage it - all vital  factors in choosing the style that's right
```

Figure 10.2 **Factors (30 random lines from the Bank of English, sorted L1)**

```
            <ZF1> are <ZF0> are on specific aspects <M01> Mm. <M02> whether it be a
     the methods <F02> Mm. <F01> and some aspects <ZF1> of <ZF0> of content and
       this decision based on commercial aspects alone is unacceptable. We strongly
                on the 14th. The best planetary aspects highlight friendships and
                 issues - it's got some serious aspects in there, but basically I wanted
              from cuttings. One of the nicest aspects of gardening is raising your own
    involvement are the most rewarding aspects of opening the NEW Legion of
             course will cover pedagogical aspects of Drama with an emphasis on
             law, socio-legal studies, legal aspects of medical practice and property
       Cash's lyrics reveal the less-cozy aspects of their relationship. Writing
  Miss Saigon, Phantom of the Opera, Aspects of Love and Cats, where a large
   12'. FADE What happens to your eyes aspects of manners in public and private
  304-7; B. F. Hoselitz, Non-Economic Aspects of Economic Growth, Glencoe, Ill.,
              they forget how to use these aspects of themselves, and helplessly sink
           of the sociological and social aspects of the problem of religion in
   the emotional, mental and spiritual aspects of our being. In order that we may
         ideas were contradictory to the aspects of Deborah he had fallen in love
      level, are in fact opposed to many aspects of perestroika but have to take
   Central Asia. But even where various aspects of civilization were available to
         issues <p> One of the most painful aspects of the diagnosis of a chronic
        shift is reflected in many different aspects of the child's life. We see it in
   extensive experience in managing all aspects of conventions and exhibitions
       has been a vocal critic of several aspects of the pay TV industry in recent
         was not capable of embracing all aspects of the inspector's decision
     s company, which means that few aspects of the club's activities are left
  committee will examine educational aspects of jazz." <M01> <tc text=Laughs>
   s the factual stuff <ZGY> biological aspects of it. Erm <tc text=pause> <M0X>
             If both positive and negative aspects test weak then either it is the
          give them a clearer idea of what aspects the department er social service
     of a chance of making the decorative aspects work. In many ways, the book is a
```

Figure 10.3 Aspects (30 random lines from the Bank of English, sorted R1)

What are corpora good for? What do (and don't) they tell us?

Corpora – or more precisely, corpus analysis methods – tell us what people usually do with language. That is, they reveal what people conventionally say and write, and how they conventionally say and write it. This perspective is very useful for a wide range of applied linguistic purposes. An obvious beneficiary is critical discourse analysis, as we saw in the example of Gabrielatos and Baker's (2008) study of newspaper representations of refugees, asylum seekers and immigrants.

It has also had a huge impact on translation work and translation studies; parallel corpora allow translators and translation studies researchers to identify translation equivalents much more efficiently than was possible in the past, and to show that translated texts have characteristic grammatical features that set them apart from both source and target language norms. Similar techniques have also had a massive impact on stylistics. It is now possible to use corpus methods to reveal the characteristic style features of an author or text. Corpus methods are now also making inroads into fields such as SLA, notably by providing psycholinguistically plausible models of how linguistic knowledge is built up by repeated encounters with certain lexical and grammatical co-occurrence patterns.

Perhaps the greatest impact thus far, however, has been on the field of foreign language teaching and the teaching of English as a foreign language in particular. This is most obviously the case with regard to commercial publications. As mentioned in Chapter 3, the first COBUILD dictionary paved the way for a revolution in the way learners' dictionaries were compiled. A similar effect has subsequently taken place in the realm of pedagogic grammars. *The Cambridge Grammar of English* (Carter and McCarthy 2006), for example, contains separate corpus-informed descriptions of spoken and written grammar, and begins with a section entirely devoted to the unique grammatical properties of a wide range of high frequency words. We have also reviewed the highly innovative 'pattern grammar' approach of Francis, Manning and Hunston (1996, 1998); here, we saw that practical corpus analysis work done as part of the COBUILD dictionary project generated an entirely new approach to grammatical description, one that has had a considerable impact on mainstream linguistics as well as on the practical domain of language pedagogy. The best-known example of a grammar reference book based entirely on the findings of corpus linguistic analyses is the *Longman Grammar of Spoken and Written English* (Biber *et al.* 1999). This volume does not present the grammar of English in monolithic terms, but shows instead how particular grammatical features vary dramatically across four different registers or varieties of English: academic prose, fiction, news and casual conversation.

Corpus analysis has also had a substantial (if somewhat less direct) impact on language teaching coursebooks and on course development. In particular, it has caused teachers, course designers and coursebook writers to pay more attention to vocabulary syllabi: the question of which words (and which combinations of words) should be taught and in what order is now a matter of central concern, and is no longer seen as an issue that can be dealt with on an ad hoc basis. Corpus analysis has also led to a new and highly welcome emphasis on register varieties. In particular, coursebooks are now beginning to appear that explicitly and exclusively attempt to teach informal conversational spoken English. Teachers are also beginning to see the benefits of learner corpus research, which (as we saw in the example of Milton's research above) has the power to reveal features of the target language that students overuse and underuse, thereby indicating areas for explicit pedagogic attention. There are now also growing numbers of books and articles that focus on helping teachers to exploit corpora in their own classrooms (e.g. Lee and Swales 2006; O'Keeffe *et al.* 2007; Reppen 2010).

What current corpora *cannot* do, however, is provide a totally accurate reflection of a living language such as English. Although corpus linguists take great care to ensure that the corpora that they build and use are representative of the language or language variety that they wish to make claims about, it must still be admitted that corpora can only represent languages and language varieties in a very modest and imperfect way. It is perhaps for this reason that Sinclair's definition quoted at the beginning of this chapter uses the word 'characteristic' instead of 'representative'. As we saw in Chapter 7, achieving representativeness in empirical research is a matter of obtaining a sample from a known population. Given that the total population of speakers and writers of English is unknown (and probably unknowable), how well does even a very large corpus such as the Bank of English, or a very carefully constructed corpus such as BNC, actually 'represent' English in this strict sense? The Bank of English is also compromised by the fact that it contains a disproportionate amount of newspaper data, while the BNC is also compromised by its dated contents, and by its emphasis on written rather than spoken language. Ninety per cent of the BNC consists of written English, and only 10 per cent consists of spoken data; these proportions are probably something like the reverse of what actually gets produced in total by speakers and writers of English around the world on any given day.

In short, if we want to use a corpus to make generalised statements about a language, these generalisations must be of a very tentative nature indeed. However, there is no doubt that it is nearly always better – qualitatively as well as quantitatively – to base such statements on a computer corpus consisting of 100,000 texts than on a physical corpus consisting of photocopies of 30 texts.

Conclusion

Corpus analysis is an increasingly basic and standard part of many forms of applied linguistic research. This being the case, some degree of familiarity with corpus tools and methods is rapidly becoming an integral part of postgraduate training. We hope that this chapter has given you some idea of what you can do with these resources, and of what these resources can do for you. We also hope to have 'demystified' corpus research for you to some degree. In our experience, many students assume that you have to be a computer programmer or an expert in statistics to do corpus linguistics, but this is very far from being the case in reality. On the contrary, you do not need any special skills whatsoever to carry out any of the analytical procedures described above – each is just a few simple mouse clicks away. Admittedly, this creates a new kind of skills problem: the software restricts what you can and cannot do with your data, which is essentially the same thing as saying that the software dictates what questions you can and cannot ask about your data. In recognition of this problem, some applied linguists go on to develop a more advanced set of skills (typically in computer programming and/or statistics) that will take them beyond this reliance on existing software. For most researchers, however, existing software is more than adequate for most research purposes, and the time and effort required to develop advanced-level skills would not be justified by improvements in research outcomes.

In any case, corpus analysis requires an even more important skill that cannot be delegated to the computer, and which cannot be acquired through technical training: the skill of interpreting. The computer can only present data to you; it cannot tell you what these data might mean, or even whether they are important or not. These analytical skills can only be developed and honed through practical experience as you progress through your studies, and are entirely reliant on you rolling up your sleeves and engaging with the data yourself.

Conclusion

In this book we hope to have provided you with some useful guidance as you commence a university programme in applied linguistics. We have looked at the sorts of topics that you are likely to cover, and we have explored some of the many different ways in which you might explore these topics through qualitative, quantitative and text-based research. We have also discussed ways in which you can usefully go about reading and writing about topics in applied linguistics. We also hope that when you reach the end of your studies, you will want to maintain some kind of involvement in applied linguistics, and that you may even feel that you would like to continue working and researching in the area. You may have written a particularly good paper that you would like to consider extending and developing so that it can be published in an academic journal, you may want to continue researching a topic that you began to study during your degree, or you may even want to go on and start a PhD in applied linguistics. In this short concluding chapter we will offer some advice about how you can get more involved in applied linguistics, how you can pursue your studies further, and most importantly, how to make your studies count.

Getting involved

Whatever path you decide to take, we hope that you will want to keep abreast of current developments in the field. One of the easiest ways to do this is to join an academic association devoted to the study of applied linguistics. The International Association of Applied Linguistics (AILA) (www.aila.info) has over 8,000 members who, according to its website, include 'researchers, policy makers and practitioners'. It publishes an annual *AILA Review* which provides state of the art perspectives on developments in the field. The three largest national academic associations for applied linguistics are the American Association for Applied Linguistics (www.aaal.org), the British Association for Applied Linguistics (www.baal.org.uk) and the Applied Linguistics Association of Australia (www.alaa.org.au). There are a number of other smaller applied linguistics associations around the world, a list of which can be found on the AILA website. Most national associations are affiliated to AILA. Similar information about applied linguistics organisations can also be found on the Linguist List website (www.linguistlist.org). The Linguist List also has a useful register of jobs in the area of applied linguistics, ongoing projects and relevant conferences, and there is also a very extensive discussion list.

Because language teaching is so closely entwined with applied linguistics it is also worth mentioning some of the larger language teaching research associations. The most well-known of these for English is Teaching English to Speakers of Other Languages or TESOL (www.tesol.org), which holds an annual conference in the USA and supports its own academic publications, the *TESOL Quarterly* and the *TESOL Journal*. TESOL has affiliates in over 45 different countries and many of these also organise their own conferences. The Modern Language Association (www.mla.org) fulfils a similar role but is concerned with a wider range of languages than TESOL.

Most applied linguistics organisations hold a conference once a year or once every two years. You do not have to present a paper to attend a conference, and it is advisable to attend a conference without giving a paper in the first instance to get an idea of what happens at these events, what is expected of conference delegates and the sorts of things that are discussed. Attending presentations by other researchers will also help you to develop a sense of what makes (and what does not make!) a good conference presentation. The larger applied linguistics associations usually have a number of smaller 'special interest groups' (SIGs) looking for example at issues such as language teaching, corpus linguistics or psycholinguistics, and newsgroups through which you can gain access to information more closely related to these specific topics and make contact with people working in these areas.

Taking it further

If you decide that you want to do a PhD in applied linguistics, the first thing you must do is to identify a research area and set of research questions. This must be something that you are very interested in as it will need to sustain your interest for at least three years. When you are designing your research questions and identifying a research area you need to think about whether there is a real need for your study both in the applied linguistics community and in the world in general. You need to identify an issue for which you can find a strong justification for investigating. The next step is to identify a suitable supervisor. If you know the area sufficiently well you should already have a good idea of who you would be interested in having as a supervisor. The best thing to do then is to familiarise yourself with the work of that particular person and then to contact them by e-mail to see if they would in principle be interested in supervising your PhD. If they are, then you would need to prepare a full PhD proposal. In such a proposal you would need to provide the background to your proposed study in which you use current literature to justify the need for such a study. You would then need to outline your main research question or questions explaining why they need to be addressed. You would also need to provide a brief outline of how you might expect to conduct the study outlining possible research methodologies that you might use and explaining why you would use them. Finally it is helpful if you can provide a proposed timeframe for the study and a set of possible predicted outcomes. On average we would expect a PhD proposal to be between 3,000 and 5,000 words. Our advice is to target a particular supervisor or a university with particular strengths in your proposed area, rather than a university that has a good reputation in general. It is important to note at this point that PhD application procedures vary greatly from university to university and between different countries. It is therefore important to find out what these procedures are with the institution where you would like to study, before beginning the application process.

Making it count

Whether or not you decide to continue with your studies, it is a good idea to make the knowledge you gained count in some way. One obvious and immediately useful way to do this is to share the knowledge that you have gained on your course with others in your workplace. You can do this by giving presentations and talks, organising study groups, and perhaps even setting up your own research or professional development initiatives, such as reviewing and revising a school curriculum, redesigning teaching materials, or trialling and evaluating new translation software. You may find that the results of such initiatives might be interesting and novel enough to report at a conference, or to write up for publication in an academic or professional journal, and you should also consider publishing your coursework if you got very high grades in your MA programme. In this regard it is worth pointing out that some of the published studies cited in this book started life as pieces of applied linguistics coursework by students of ours.

But if you do aim to publish your work, you will almost certainly need to revise it (and often very substantially) before it will be accepted for publication in a journal. There are a number of important differences between postgraduate essays and dissertations on the one hand and journal articles on the other, and you need to bear in mind that revising is hard work! You should also be aware that it is very rare for submitted work to be accepted without any revisions, and it is quite normal for a paper to be rejected outright. If this happens to you, our advice is to keep at it – use the critical feedback that you will have received on your draft submission to improve your work, and then resubmit it to the same journal or to another one if the first journal has explicitly asked you not to resubmit to them. Other ways to get involved include writing letters to newspapers and magazines, blogging and attending public debates where language problems are a central concern.

Final thoughts

Applied linguistics is still a comparatively young field, so by doing applied linguistics you will be helping to shape its future development. Where once applied linguistics was the preserve of a fairly small group of people working on a fairly restricted set of topics, it has now become a much more wide-ranging field which encompasses researchers who are working on very different problems, questions and issues. What this means for you is that there has never been a more exciting time to do applied linguistics than the present! We hope that this small book will have helped you to set off on your own journey into this fascinating subject, and that you will want to get involved, take it further and make it count as an applied linguist yourself.

Appendix 1

Major journals in applied linguistics and related fields

- *AILA Review*
- *Applied Linguistics*
- *Applied Psycholinguistics*
- *Annual Review of Applied Linguistics*
- *Babel*
- *The Canadian Modern Language Review*
- *Corpora*
- *Corpus Linguistics and Linguistic Theory*
- *Critical Discourse Studies*
- *Discourse and Society*
- *Discourse Studies*
- *ELT Journal*
- *English for Specific Purposes*
- *Functions of Language*
- *International Journal of Applied Linguistics*
- *International Journal of Corpus Linguistics*
- *International Journal of Lexicography*
- *International Journal of Speech, Language and the Law*
- *International Review of Applied Linguistics*
- *Issues in Applied Linguistics*
- *Journal of English for Academic Purposes*
- *Journal of Intercultural Communication*
- *Journal of Pragmatics*

- Journal of Sociolinguistics
- *Language Awareness*
- *Language and Society*
- *Language Learning*
- *Language Teaching*
- *Language Teaching Research*
- *Language Testing*
- Linguistics and Education
- The Modern Language Journal
- *ReCALL Journal*
- RELC Journal
- *Studies in Second Language Acquisition*
- *System*
- *Target*
- TESOL Quarterly
- Text and Talk
- *Written Communication*

A comprehensive, up-to-date annotated list of Applied Linguistics journals, containing links to the journals' websites can be found on the Linguist List website: http://linguistlist.org/pubs/journals/browse-journals.cfm.

Appendix 2

Suggestions for further reading

Chapter 1

For a comprehensive overview of the field

Davies, A. and Elder, C. (eds) (2006) The Handbook of Applied Linguistics, Oxford: Blackwell.

Johnson, K. and Johnson, H. (1999) The Encyclopedic Dictionary of Applied Linguistics: A Handbook for Language Teaching (Blackwell Handbooks in Linguistics), Oxford: Blackwell.

Kaplan, R.B. (2005) (ed.) The Oxford Handbook of Applied Linguistics (Oxford Handbooks in Linguistics), New York: Oxford University Press.

In-depth introductions

Coffin, C., Lillis, T. and O'Halloran, K. (2009) Applied Linguistics Methods: A Reader, Abingdon: Routledge.

Cook, G. and North, S. (2010) Applied Linguistics in Action: A Reader, London: Routledge.

Davies, A. (2007) An Introduction to Applied Linguistics: From Practice to Theory, second edition, Edinburgh: Edinburgh University Press.

Hunston, S. and Oakey, D. (eds) (2009) *Introducing Applied Linguistics*, Abingdon: Routledge.

Paltridge, B. and Phakiti, A. (eds) (2010) *Continuum Companion to Research Methods in Applied Linguistics*, London: Continuum.

Schmitt, N. (2010) *An Introduction to Applied Linguistics*, second edition. London: Hodder Education.

Critical perspectives

McCarthy, M. (2001) *Issues in Applied Linguistics*, Cambridge: Cambridge University Press.

Seidlhofer, B. (2003) *Controversies in Applied Linguistics*, Oxford: Oxford University Press.

Detailed definitions of key terms in applied linguistics

Richards, J., Schmidt, D., Platt, H. and Schmitt, M. (2002) *The Longman Dictionary of Language Teaching and Applied Linguistics*, third edition, Harlow: Longman.

Chapter 2

Language teaching methodology

Richards, J.C. and Renandya, W. (2002) *Methodology in Language Teaching: An Anthology of Current Practice*, Cambridge: Cambridge University Press.

Richards, J.C. and Rodgers, T. (2001) *Approaches and Methods in Language Teaching*, second edition, Cambridge: Cambridge University Press.

Syllabus and materials design

Tomlinson, B. (1998) *Developing Materials for Language Teaching*, Cambridge: Cambridge University Press.

McGrath, I. (2002) *Materials Evaluation and Design for Language Teaching*, Edinburgh: Edinburgh University Press.

Language testing

Bachman, L.F. and Palmer, S. (1996) Language Testing in Practice, Oxford: Oxford University Press.

Hughes, A. (2003) Testing for Language Teachers, second edition, Cambridge: Cambridge University Press.

English for specific purposes

Dudley-Evans, T. and St John, M. (1998) Developments in English for Specific Purposes, Cambridge: Cambridge University Press.

Hyland, K. (2006) English for Academic Purposes, Abingdon: Routledge.

Koester, A. (2006) Investigating Workplace Discourse, Abingdon: Routledge.

Second language acquisition

Ellis, R. (2008) The Study of Second Language Acquisition, Oxford: Oxford University Press.

Mitchell, R. and Myles, F. (2004) Second Language Learning Theories, London: Blackwell.

Psycholinguistics

Field, J. (2003) Psycholinguistics: A Resource Book for Students, London: Routledge.

Language policy and planning

Ferguson, G. (2006).Language Planning in Education, Edinburgh: Edinburgh University Press.

Skutnabb-Kangas, T. (2000) Linguistic Genocide in Education – Or Worldwide Diversity and Human Rights? Mahwah, NJ: Lawrence Erlbaum Associates.

Tollefson, J. (1991) Planning Language, Planning Inequality, London: Longman.

Tollefson, J. (2002) Language Policies in Education. Critical Issues, Mahwah, NJ: Lawrence Erlbaum Associates.

Forensic linguistics

Coulthard, R.M. and Johnson, A. (2007) *An Introduction to Forensic Linguistics: Language in Evidence*, London: Routledge.

Gibbons, J. (2003) *Forensic Linguistics: An Introduction to Language in the Justice System*, Oxford: Blackwell.

Critical discourse analysis

Fairclough, N. (2010) *Critical Discourse Analysis: The Critical Study of Language*, Harlow: Longman.

Wodak, R. and Meyer, M. (2009) *Methods of Critical Discourse Analysis*, London: Sage Publications.

Translation studies

Hatim, B. and Munday, J. (2004) *Translation: An Advanced Resource Book*, London: Routledge.

Lexicography

Jackson, H. (2002) *Lexicography: An Introduction*, London: Routledge.

Generative grammar

Cook, V. and Newson, M. (2007) *Chomsky's Universal Grammar: An Introduction*, London: Blackwell.

Systemic-functional linguistics

Eggins, S. (2004) *An Introduction to Systemic Functional Linguistics*, London: Continuum.

Halliday, M.A.K. and Matthiessen, C.M.I.M. (2004) *An Introduction to Functional Grammar*, third edition, London: Arnold.

Cognitive linguistics

Evans, V. and Green, M. (2006) *Cognitive Linguistics: An Introduction*, Edinburgh: Edinburgh University Press.

Lee, D. (2001) *Cognitive Linguistics: An Introduction*, Oxford: Oxford University Press.

Littlemore, J. (2009) *Applying Cognitive Linguistics to Second Language Learning and Teaching*, Basingstoke: Palgrave Macmillan.

Ungerer, F. and Schmid, H.J. (2006) *An Introduction to Cognitive Linguistics*, second edition, Harlow: Pearson Longman.

Chapter 3

Communicative language teaching

Brown, H.D. (2007) *Principles and Practice in Language Teaching*, London: Longman.

Cook, V. (2008) *Second Language Learning and Language Teaching*, fourth revised edition, London: Hodder Education.

Hedge, T. (2000) *Teaching and Learning in the Language Classroom*, Oxford: Oxford University Press.

Widdowson, H. (2003), *Defining Issues in English Language Teaching*, Oxford: Oxford University Press.

Language change

Aitchison, J. (2001) *Language Change: Progress or Decay?* Oxford: Oxford University Press.

Vague language

Channell, J. (2003) *Vague Language*, Oxford: Oxford University Press.

Chapter 4

Bailey, S. (2006) *Academic Writing: A Handbook for International Students*, second edition, Abingdon: Routledge.

Bitchener, J. (2010) *Writing an Applied Linguistics Thesis or Dissertation*, Basingstoke: Palgrave Macmillan.

Ridley, D. (2008) *The Literature Review: A Step-by-Step Guide for Students*, London: Sage.

Wallace, M. and Wray, A. (2011) *Critical Reading and Writing for Postgraduates*, second edition, London: Sage.

Chapters 5 and 6

Cameron, D. (2001) *Working with Spoken Discourse*, London: Sage Publications.

Dörnyei, Z. (2007) *Research Methods in Applied Linguistics*, Oxford: Oxford University Press.

Eggins, S. and Slade, D. (2005) *Analysing Everyday Conversation*, London: Equinox.

Perry, F. (2005) *Research in Applied Linguistics: Becoming a Discerning Consumer*, Abingdon: Routledge.

Chapters 7 and 8

Dörnyei, Z. (2007) *Research Methods in Applied Linguistics*, Oxford: Oxford University Press.

Gries, S.T. (2009) *Statistics for Linguistics with R: A Practical Introduction*. Berlin: Mouton de Gruyter.

Larson-Hall, J. (2009) *A Guide to Doing Statistics in Second Language Research Using SPSS*, Abingdon: Routledge.

Pallant, J. (2005) *SPSS Survival Manual: A Step-by-Step Guide to Using SPSS*, Maidenhead: Open University Press.

Rasinger, S.M. (2008) *Quantitative Research in Linguistics: An Introduction*, London: Continuum.

Chapter 9

Coffin, C., Donohue, J. and North, S. (2009) *Exploring English Grammar: From Formal to Functional*, London: Routledge.

Cutting, J. (2007) *Pragmatics and Discourse: A Resource Book for Students*, London: Routledge.

Gee, J.P. (2011) *An Introduction to Discourse Analysis*, London: Routledge.

Hoey, M. (2001) *Textual Interaction: An Introduction to Written Discourse Analysis*, London: Routledge.

Jaworski, A. and Coupland, N. (eds) (2006) *The Discourse Reader*, second edition, London: Routledge.

Johnstone, B. (2008) *Discourse Analysis*, second edition, Oxford: Blackwell.

McCarthy, M. (2001) *Discourse Analysis for Language Teachers*, Cambridge: Cambridge University Press.

Schiffrin, D., Tannen, D. and Hamilton, H. (eds) (2003) *Handbook of Discourse Analysis*, Oxford: Blackwell.

Chapter 10

Biber, D., Conrad, S. and Reppen, R. (1998) *Corpus Linguistics: Investigating Language Structure and Use*, Cambridge: Cambridge University Press.

Bondi, M. and Scott, M. (2010) *Keyness in Texts*, Amsterdam/Philadelphia, PA: John Benjamins.

Hunston, S. (2002) *Corpora in Applied Linguistics*, Cambridge: Cambridge University Press.

Kennedy, G. (1998) *An Introduction to Corpus Linguistics*, Harlow: Longman.

McEnery, T., Xiao, R. and Tono, Y. (2006) *Corpus-Based Language Studies: An Advanced Resource Book*, Abingdon: Routledge.

Notes

Chapter 1

1   See 'No more loose talk' at:
    www.guardian.co.uk/uk/2004/nov/06/britishidentity.comment.

Chapter 8

1   A sample of a Modern Language Aptitude Test can be found at:
    www.2lti.com/htm/Test_mlat.pdf.

Chapter 9

1   Moore's original example numbers have been changed to fit the
    numbering system used in this chapter.

Chapter 10

1   Available at: www.ota.ahds.ac.uk.
2   Available at: www.elicorpora.info.
3   Available at: http://davies-linguistics.byu.edu/personal.
4   Available at: www.sketchengine.co.uk.

References

Ädel, A. (2010) Group talk in educational settings: a corpus-based study of rapport-building language use, paper presented at *ICAME 31: Corpus Linguistics and Variation in English*, Justus Liebig University, Giessen, Germany, 29 May 2010.

Bachman, L. (1990) *Fundamental Considerations in Language Testing*, New York: Oxford University Press.

Biber, D., Finegan, E., Johansson, S. and Conrad, S. (1999) *The Longman Grammar of Spoken and Written English*, London: Longman.

Boers, F. (1997) No pain no gain in a free-market rhetoric: a test for cognitive semantics? *Metaphor and Symbol*, 12(4): 231–241.

Boers, F. and Demecheleer, M. (1995) Travelers, patients and warriors in English, Dutch and French economic discourse, *Revue Belge de Philosophie et de l'Histoire*, 73(3): 673–691.

Borg, S. and Burns, A. (2008) Integrating grammar in adult TESOL classrooms, *Applied Linguistics*, 29(3): 456–482.

Bressem, J. (2008) *Notating Gestures – Proposal for a Form Based Notation System of Coverbal Gestures*, unpublished manuscript, online, available at: www.janabressem.de/Downloads/Bressem_notating gestures.pdf.

Brumfit, C. (1995) Teacher professionalism and research, in G. Cook and B. Seidlhofer (eds), *Principle and Practice in Applied Linguistics*, Oxford: Oxford University Press, pp. 27–41.

Brumfit, C. and Johnson, K. (eds) (1979) *The Communicative Approach to Language Teaching*, Oxford: Oxford University Press.

Bygate, M., Skehan, P. and Swain, M. (2009) *Researching Pedagogic Tasks: Second Language Learning, Teaching and Testing*, London: Longman.

Bylund, E., Abrahamson, N. and Hyltenstam, K. (2009) The role of language aptitude in first language attrition: the case of pre-pubescent attriters, *Applied Linguistics*, 31(3): 443–464.

Cameron, L. (2008) Metaphor shifting in the dynamics of talk, in M.S. Zanotto, L. Cameron and M.C. Cavalcanti (eds), *Confronting Metaphor in Use: An Applied Linguistic Approach*, Amsterdam: John Benjamins.

Canale M. and Swain M. (1980) Theoretical bases of communicative approaches to second language teaching and testing, *Applied Linguistics*, 1(1): 1–47.

Carter, R. and McCarthy, M. (1997) *Exploring Spoken English*, Cambridge: Cambridge University Press.

Carter, R. and McCarthy, M. (2006) *Cambridge Grammar of English: A Comprehensive Guide to Spoken and Written English Grammar and Usage*. Cambridge: Cambridge University Press.

Chafe, W. (1993) Prosodic and functional units of language, in J. Edwards and M. Lampert (eds), *Talking Data: Transcription and Coding in Discourse Research*, Mahwah, NJ: Lawrence Erlbaum Associates.

Clark, K. (1992) The linguistics of blame, in M. J. Toolan (ed.), *Language, Text and Context*, London: Routledge, pp. 208–224.

Cook, G. (2004) *Genetically Modified Language*, Abingdon: Routledge.

Coulthard, M. (1994) Powerful evidence for the defence: an exercise in forensic discourse analysis, in J. Gibbons (ed.), *Language and the Law*, Harlow: Longman, pp. 414–427.

De Ridder, I., Vangehuchten, L. and Sesena Gomez, M. (2007) Enhancing automaticity through task-based learning, *Applied Linguistics*, 28(2): 309–315.

Derwing, T., Munro, M. and Thompson, R. (2007), A longitudinal study of ESL learners' fluency and comprehensibility development, *Applied Linguistics*, 29(3): 359–380.

Dörnyei, Z. (2003) *Questionnaires in Second Language Research: Construction, Administration, and Processing*, Mahwah, NJ: Lawrence Erlbaum Associates.

Dörnyei, Z. (2007) *Research Methods in Applied Linguistics*, Oxford: Oxford University Press.

Eagleson, R. (1994) Forensic analysis of personal written text: a case study, in J. Gibbons (ed.), *Language and the Law*, Harlow: Longman, pp. 362–373.

Ehrman, M. (1996) *Understanding Second Language Learning Difficulties*, Thousand Oaks, CA: Sage.

Ellis, R. and Barkhuizen, G. (2005) *Analysing Learner Language*, Oxford: Oxford University Press.

Fairclough, N. (2003) *Analysing Discourse: Textual Analysis for Social Research*, London: Routledge.

Francis, G., Manning, E. and Hunston, S. (1996) *Collins COBUILD Grammar Patterns 1:Verbs*, London: HarperCollins.

Francis, G., Manning, E. and Hunston, S. (1998) *Collins COBUILD Grammar Patterns 2: Nouns and Adjectives*, London: HarperCollins.

Gabrielatos, C. and Baker, P. (2008) Fleeing, sneaking, flooding: a corpus analysis of discursive constructions of refugees and asylum seekers in the UK press, 1996–2005, *Journal of English Linguistics*, 36(1) 5–38.

Grinsted, A. (1997) Joking as a strategy in Spanish and Danish negotiations, in F. Bargiela-Chiappini and S. Harris (eds), *The Languages of Business: An International Perspective*, Edinburgh: Edinburgh University Press, pp. 159–182.

Groom, N. (2000) Attribution and averral revisited: three perspectives on manifest intertextuality in academic writing, in P. Thompson (ed.), *Patterns and Perspectives: Insights into EAP Writing Practice*, Reading: University of Reading, pp. 14–25.

Groom, N. (2007) *Phraseology and Epistemology in Humanities Writing: A Corpus-Driven Study*, PhD thesis, University of Birmingham.

Halliday, M.A.K. (1994) *An Introduction to Functional Grammar*, second edition, London: Edward Arnold.

Halliday, M.A.K. and Matthiessen, C.M.I.M. (2004) *An Introduction to Functional Grammar*, third edition, London: Arnold.

Hedge, T. (2000) *Teaching and Learning in the Language Classroom*, Oxford: Oxford University Press.

Hsiao, T-Y. and Oxford, R. (2002) Comparing theories of language learning strategies: a confirmatory factor analysis, *The Modern Language Journal*, 86(3): 368–383.

Hunston, S. (2002) *Corpora in Applied Linguistics*, Cambridge: Cambridge University Press.

Hutchby, I. and Wooffit, R. (2008) *Conversation Analysis*, second edition, Cambridge: Polity Press.

Jenkins, J. and Seidlhofer, B. (2001) Teaching English as a lingua franca for Europe, *Guardian Weekly*, 18 April.

Kasper, G. and Roever, C. (2005) Pragmatics in second language learning, in E. Hinkel (ed.), *Handbook of Research in Second Language Teaching and Learning*, Mahwah, NJ: Lawrence Erlbaum Associates.

Koester, A. (2004) Relational sequences in workplace genres, *Journal of Pragmatics*, 36(8): 1405–1428.

Koester, A., Pitt, A., Handford, M. and Lisboa, M. (forthcoming) *Business Advantage Intermediate*, Cambridge: Cambridge University Press.

Larson-Hall, J. (2009) *A Guide to Doing Statistics in Second Language Research Using SPSS*, Abingdon: Routledge.

Lee, D. and Swales, J.M. (2006) A corpus-based EAP course for NNS doctoral students: moving from available specialized corpora to self-compiled corpora, *English for Specific Purposes*, 25(1): 56–75.

Littlemore, J. (2001) Learning styles and learning strategies in second language acquisition, *Perspectives*, 27(2): 7–18.

Littlemore, J., Tang, P., Chen, P., Barnden, J. and Koester, A. (2010) The role of figurative thinking in gaining access to discourse communities: a report on two case studies, in S. De Knop, F. Boers and T. De Rycker (eds), *Exploring the Lexis-Grammar Continuum in Second Language Pedagogy* (Applications of Cognitive Linguistics), Berlin: Mouton de Gruyter, pp. 189–211.

Matsumoto, Y. (2009) From the old to the new paradigm of teaching: the impact of group dynamics of the teachers and students in Japanese University ELT classrooms, *Bulletin of Kiryu University, Japan*, 21, online, available at: www.ukm.my/solls09/Proceeding/PDF/Yasuyo.pdf.

Milton, J. (1998) Exploiting L1 and interlanguage corpora in the design of an electronic language learning and production environment, in S. Granger (ed.), *Learner English on Computer*, Harlow: Longman, pp. 186–198.

Moore, T. (2002) Knowledge and agency: a study of metaphenomenal discourse in textbooks from three disciplines, *English for Specific Purposes*, 21(4): 347–366.

Myers, G. (1995) From discovery to invention: the writing and rewriting of two patents, *Social Studies of Science*, 25(1): 57–105.

Nakatani, Y. (2005) The effects of awareness-raising training on oral communication strategy use, *The Modern Language Journal*, 89(1): 76–91.

Nunan, D. (2004) *Task-Based Language Teaching*, Cambridge: Cambridge University Press.

O'Halloran, K. (2003) *Critical Discourse Analysis and Language Cognition*, Edinburgh: Edinburgh University Press.

O'Keeffe, A., McCarthy, M.J. and Carter, R.A. (2007) *From Corpus to Classroom: Language Use and Language Teaching*, Cambridge: Cambridge University Press.

Olsson, J. (2009) *Wordcrime: Solving Crime Through Forensic Linguistics*, London: Continuum.

Ormeno, V. (2009) *Metacognitive Awareness-Raising in EFL Teacher Education with Special Reference to the Chilean Context*, PhD thesis, University of Birmingham.

Pallant, J. (2005) *SPSS Survival Manual: A Step-by-Step Guide to Using SPSS*, Maidenhead: Open University Press.

Pennycook, A. (2004) Critical applied linguistics, in A. Davies and C. Elder (eds), *The Handbook of Applied Linguistics*, Oxford: Blackwell, pp. 784–807.

Poupore, G. (2008) Socio-affective aspects of small group EFL tasks: motivation, group dynamic and the effect of task topic, unpublished PhD dissertation, University of Birmingham.

Poupore, G. (forthcoming) Socio-affective aspects of small group EFL tasks: motivation, group dynamic and the effect of task topic, *Language Teaching Research*.

Reppen, R. (2010) *Using Corpora in the Language Classroom*, Cambridge: Cambridge University Press.

Richards, J.C. and Rodgers, T. (2001) *Approaches and Methods in Language Teaching*, second edition, Cambridge: Cambridge University Press.

Richards, J.C., Platt, J. and Platt, H. (1992) *The Longman Dictionary of Applied Linguistics*, London: Longman.

Richards, J.C, Schmidt, D., Platt, H. and Schmitt, M. (2002) *The Longman Dictionary of Language Teaching and Applied Linguistics*, third edition, Harlow: Longman.

Richards, K. and Seedhouse, P. (eds) (2007) *Applying Conversation Analysis*, London: Palgrave Macmillan.

Ridley, D. (2008) *The Literature Review: A Step-by-Step Guide for Students*, London: Sage.

Roberts, C., Sarangi, S. and Moss, B. (2004) Presentation of self and symptoms in primary care consultations involving patients from non-English speaking backgrounds, *Communication and Medicine*, 1(2): 159–169.

Rodgers, D. (1997) *English for International Negotiations. A Cross-Cultural Case Study Approach*, Cambridge: Cambridge University Press.

Seedhouse, P. (1999) Task-based interaction, *ELT Journal*, 53(3): 149–156.

Seedhouse, P. (2004) *The Interactional Architecture of the Language Classroom: A Conversation Analysis Perspective*, Malden, MA: Blackwell.

Seidlhofer, B. (2005) English as a lingua franca, *ELT Journal*, 59(4): 339–341.

Sinclair, J. (1991) *Corpus, Concordance, Collocation: Describing English Language*, Oxford: Oxford University Press.

Skehan, P. (1998) *A Cognitive Approach to Language Learning*, Oxford: Oxford University Press.

Slobin, D. (2003) Language and thought online: cognitive consequences of linguistic relativity, in D. Gentner and S. Goldin-Meadow (eds), *Language in Mind: Advances in the Study of Language and Thought*, Cambridge, MA: MIT Press, pp. 157–192.

Swales, J.M. (1990) *Genre Analysis: English in Academic and Research Settings*, Cambridge: Cambridge University Press.

Tagg, C. (2009) *A Corpus Linguistics Study of SMS Text Messaging*, unpublished PhD thesis, University of Birmingham.

Tatsumoto, M. (2010) *The Effects of Cooperative Learning on Student Motivation in the Japanese University EFL Classroom*, PhD thesis, University of Birmingham.

ten Have, P. (2007) *Doing Conversation Analysis: A Practical Guide*, second edition, London: Sage.

Tognini-Bonelli, E. (2001) *Corpus Linguistics at Work*, Amsterdam: John Benjamins.

Vidal, K. (2003) Academic listening: a source of vocabulary acquisition? *Applied Linguistics*, 24(1): 56–89.

Viney, P. and Viney, K. (1996) *Handshake: A Course in Communication*, Oxford: Oxford University Press.

Widdowson, H.G. (1978) *Teaching Language as Communication*, Oxford: Oxford University Press.

Widdowson, H.G. (2004) *Text, Context, Pretext: Critical Issues in Discourse Analysis*, Oxford: Blackwell.

Willis, D. (1990) *The Lexical Syllabus: A New Approach to Language Teaching*, London: Collins COBUILD.

Yu, G. (2009) Lexical diversity in writing and speaking task performances, *Applied Linguistics*, 31(2): 236–259.

Index